D1602526

THESE ISLANDS,
WE SING

These Islands, We Sing

An Anthology of Scottish Islands Poetry

Edited by

Kevin MacNeil

First published in Great Britain in 2011
by Polygon, an imprint of Birlinn Ltd

Birlinn Ltd
West Newington House
10 Newington Road
Edinburgh EH9 1QS

www.polygonbooks.co.uk

ISBN   978 1 84697 196 9

British Library Cataloguing-in-Publication Data
A catalogue record for this book is available
on request from the British Library.

The publisher gratefully acknowledges funding
from these organisations.

Typeset in Great Britain by Antony Gray
Printed and bound by   Grafica veneta, Italy

For my mother and father,
born and raised on separate islands,
and
for Charlotte,
new to Scottish island culture

Contents

Introduction

Poetry is often perceived as a difficult or intimidating art form. Partly, I think, because it demands our full attention, body and mind; we need to immerse ourselves in it. Yet, surely, when carefully considered, this is very positive. Life itself is composed of moments, and the intensification of these makes our experience of it richer and more fulfilling. Coupled with the insights good poetry offers to us or elicits from us, reading or writing it is useful and life-enhancing. Poetry, as T. S. Eliot said, is 'not the assertion that something is true, but the making of that truth more fully real to us'.

Poetry is grossly undervalued today, and even dedicated readers sometimes overlook the disproportionate excellence of 20th- and 21st-century poetry from the Scottish isles: a strange confluence of self-defeating injustices. I believe this is the first poetry anthology of its kind – that is, one with a remit wide enough to bring in writing from any Scottish island, but distinct enough not to include Highland or other mainland work.

It is self-evidently worthwhile to take stock of who we are, to boost our understanding of how and why we exist, and to appreciate, through potent empathy, the actions of others. Poetry, which helps us with all of these things, is nourishing both intellectually and emotionally. 'A poem,' says Serbian-American writer Charles Simic, 'is an instant of lucidity in which the entire organism participates.' No wonder, then, that the making, performing and hearing of poetry lies at the heart of so many religions. Poetry's efficacy, like its non-material cost, can be extraordinary.

During periods of recession we realise how transitory are those material things which contemporary Western society so clamorously promotes. In times of economic distress we turn to each other. We share. And we realise that we have a powerful foundation in the best uses of our various languages. In poetry we find mirrors, paintings, hugs, scoldings, witnesses, oracles, lies, intimacy, resilience, altruism, self-absorption, pride, humility, truth, solitude, communion, every physical and abstract thing. We owe so much to literature, this humane miracle that enriches actual lives.

And yet, as I write, libraries and bookshops across the country are dying, or being actively killed off. Such losses are astonishing and, in some cases, iniquitous. As digital technology advances, many believe the existence of the book as we know it is under threat.

Poetry is tenacious, however; it will survive cutbacks, political impediments and, in all its senses, ignorance. Freud, who was awarded the Goethe Prize for his contribution to German literary culture (and whose books were burned by the Nazis), said: 'Beauty has no obvious use; nor is there any clear cultural necessity for it. Yet civilisation could not do without it.'

Is poetry, as cynics complain, elitist? At best it is quite the opposite – as I hope this collection demonstrates. Historically, poetry, often in the form of prayer or song, was a daily part of island life. Many of the mundane tasks men and women performed were subject to shared rhythms (for example, waulking tweed, rowing or spinning wool), and, to augment these rhythms and lighten the workload, songs were routinely sung, further bonding the islanders in their sharing of lyrics and interpretation of themes, and events. Islanders had an overt, practical need of poetry – but they also used it for entertainment, for reinforcing their history and for expressing who they were. Poetry was anything but elitist; it was commonplace.

And it is still relevant today. I believe the poetry in this anthology is among the best that the UK has produced since the start of the twentieth century. Even the most objective critic will appreciate that a high proportion of the finest and most important poets of recent years have had a connection with one or other of the Scottish isles: Sorley MacLean, George Mackay Brown, Iain Crichton Smith, Edwin Muir, Hugh MacDiarmid. And though all those 'big' names are male, I hope this collection will go some way to remedying that gender imbalance, as it also showcases the strength of the great female island voices, so often underrated.

Many's the time, living and working on the various islands, I have heard a turn of phrase which was pitch-perfect, eloquent, ingenious – all the more so for being uttered with a natural spontaneity by someone who hadn't wittingly read a poem since school. Tone, mood, rhythm, pitch, pace and texture are aspects of language most people utilise without consciously being aware of it, and perhaps those from a traditionally oral culture are naturally more likely to unlock little quickfire linguistic seren-dipities. I remember a conversation I once had with a colleague in Skye. He said that, when he first moved to the island (from England), he was astounded by what he heard in the streets of Portree, and dashed to the nearest phone box to call his family. 'You won't believe this,' he told them, 'but the people here don't talk to each other in the streets. They *sing* to each other.'

I have written elsewhere about the inherent acoustic beauties of Gaelic, with its melodic cadences and long, flowing vowels – and the other languages of the isles are as lovely. The Shetland dialect, as the locals call it, is a fascinating blend of Norn, English and Lowland Scots. Living in Shetland was an edifying experience. I saw similarities to my home island of Lewis, but I also felt the cultural differences keenly, and had to make an active effort to tune in to the native tongue as both listener and reader. I felt warmly welcomed as an outsider, but an outsider nonetheless – which gave me a stronger empathy for incomers to Lewis.

As new people – Indian, Chinese, English, East European – come to the isles and enrich the indigenous cultures, so too the old cycle of exile continues. The islander's relationship to the mainland and other 'foreign' places is evoked by the late George Mackay Brown in a typically poetic piece of prose:

In Orkney every face has its own meaning and its own value. But here the thousands of faces that pass you in the street every hour of every day are merely flickering shadows. You see occasionally a beautiful face or a compassionate face or a suffering face; but before you can let it soak into your mind it has vanished forever in the torrent of humanity. For the most part, however, the faces lack any personality. Modern life has set its unvarying pattern to them; to the Orkneyman they seem curiously hard and unfeeling – a long endless succession of flickering shadows.

In the islands we like our 'torrent of humanity' in small, manageable pieces. That said, the islander is often well aware of the adage about familiarity and contempt. Liminality is a native state that can become deeply unsettling, yet may also catalyse the tensions that lead to the writing of poetry. I'll balance the passage quoted above with another wonderful George Mackay Brown quotation: 'No man is an island, and all that we ever say or think or do – however seemingly unremarkable – may yet set the whole web of existence trembling and affect the living and the dead and the unborn.'

An insular environment often provides a mind with ample opportunity to indulge in close, creative reading. Interminable-seeming wet weather and a sense of claustrophobia will compel some islanders to find escapism between the near-infinite covers of a book. And so we confirm that literature can take us beyond the limited shores of our own experience and provide us with a sense of enlightenment, of the inexpressible expressed in a most sublime manner. Each time a person is moved by their encounter with a poem, a unique concatenation of events takes place, and, as the poem itself is refreshed, so the reader is newly enriched with the sense of something communicated personally, one individual to another, across time and space to the here and now. This makes for a special relationship between writer and reader, a more equal one than is commonly supposed. As Borges once wrote: 'I sometimes think that good readers are poets as singular, and as awesome, as great authors themselves.'

The islands have indeed produced and attracted an inordinate number of talented poets, and it is worth considering some further reasons for this happy circumstance. Writing, it is often remarked, is the most solitary of the arts. Islands, likewise, tend to be relatively solitary places. (It is a triumph that great writers are outward-looking, not just absorbed in their own internal matters; the same is true of islands.) As the critic Wilbur Scott said: 'Art is not created in a vacuum, it is the work not simply of a person, but of an author fixed in time and space, answering a community of which he is an important, because articulate, part.'

Though it seems paradoxical to say so, liminality is a central issue. Being whaur extremes meet. The edge is the point at which the known becomes the unknown, where everything can change, and can do so quite completely. As with thrashing tide meeting solid land, the periphery is a place where opposites clash or converge, where creativity and danger are at their most alive. If Scotland's islands are seen as remote, this is because of the way their perception is mediated through dominant, often indifferent, centres of power (which are, themselves, remote when viewed from an island context). Perhaps the sense of being 'other' so often foisted upon the islander is, in the end, a problem that can become a solution, in the artist's hands, at least. The islander's sense of being removed from the heart of things (the centres of power, influence, visibility, enhanced opportunity) relates, I think, to the writer's sense of being an observer as much as a participant.

The islander's tendency towards self-deprecation has no doubt held him/her back from larger readerships. As has the distrust some insular cultures foster towards the arts, perhaps through fundamentalist dogma. Still, there is no one less defeatist than a writer. Try as some might to accentuate (subtly or otherwise) the notion that the poet is doing something frivolous or privileged or unimportant, Scottish island poetry, as this book proves, is of enormous relevance.

The corollary is that poetry's success is prose's loss. The islands have produced comparatively few novelists. This could perhaps be attributed to social issues, such as the historical predominance of song and oral storytelling and the formerly enduring perception that novels were a middle-class indulgence. In recent times we have seen exceptional novelists emerge from the Scottish islands; but they are just that – exceptions. And they are, for the most part, writers who began their publishing careers in poetry.

Writing is more than the hungry scratching of a pen or the restless prodding at a keyboard. Writing is questing. Writing is freedom. It is an escape from an insular context; one's inner life can be vastly more dynamic than the outer, especially when the outer life is rendered static by grey weather, wearying routine and sheer grinding contingency. To create something of public value is very often proof that one cares. This can only be a good thing. Therefore, in devaluing poetry, society devalues itself.

If you live on an island (and especially if you write in a minority language) your immediate readership and audience are limited. And, while the close daily connections with others may be very welcome, writing in an insular community can have the detrimental effect of making a person feel hemmed in, overly scrutinised, prodded towards conformity.

Some islanders have found that only in pushing against the tight-knit parameters of conservative uniformity and banality could they become writers. Thus their writing is apt wilfully to tend towards being fresh, engaging, exciting. But Scottish island poets are the sidelined of the sidelined. To the wider UK media and education system, the islander exists as an afterthought, if at all. This would be more understandable if the quality of writing did not make a mockery of such unfairness. As this book demonstrates, the archipelago of Scottish island literature is flourishing with poetic talent.

Growing up in Stornoway, I sometimes wondered if my island were, to the rest of the world, a mere crumb on the map. Were we an irrelevance? My passion for books aside, I'd say my saving grace was a degree in Scottish Ethnology from the University of Edinburgh's School of Scottish Studies; that M.A. was the closest I could get to an actual degree certificate from the University of Life. (The Scottish element is comparative rather than restrictive; ethnology is as intimate as a gesture, as all-encompassing as a religious faith.) I learned that my cultural background did exist, that my people did have a history, and that voices like mine were as important as anyone else's, even if fellow Scots in Edinburgh would frown at my accent and ask which country I came from. Although I have harboured many ambivalences about who and what I am over the years, I have learned that, at the very least, I can write and read my way through such issues.

In choosing the poems for this anthology, I decided that the overall governing factor had to be quality, not tokenism (of gender, class etc.) Taste is so subjective as to be potentially divisive. I trust the reader will agree that no book – least of all an anthology – can please everyone equally. After all, even the definition of an island is fluid. The General Register Office for Scotland defines an island as 'a mass of land surrounded by water, separate from the Scottish mainland'. But where does this leave the Isle of Skye, which is attached to the mainland by a bridge? And what about islands which are no longer islands at low tide? Many land masses defy categorisation. But then, so do many poems.

Scotland has about 800 offshore islands, 94 of which are inhabited and only 14 of which have a population of 1,000 or more. It stands to reason that the islands with greater populations, such as Lewis and Shetland, will be more likely to produce a larger number of poets. Some of the smaller islands have yet to develop important contemporary poetic voices, but I trust (and hope) that, in time, they will.

The project would rapidly have become unworkable if I hadn't imposed certain limitations. I decided to begin with what one might loosely call 'modern' poetry. I opted for work which added vitality to the various island literary traditions, arguably at the risk of omitting some perfectly nice poems which nonetheless offered nothing sufficiently fresh and vibrant to merit inclusion. I decided to avoid publishing work by poets who made fleeting visits to the islands, no matter how well known those writers were. This, I submit, is excusable for two reasons. Firstly, a brief visit to an island does not grant sufficient time to absorb the deeper realities of island life. Secondly, island writers – many of whom are sadly accustomed to being ignored – do not deserve to be elbowed out of their own dedicated anthology. I therefore limited eligibility to those who either grew up on or otherwise chose to live on an island.

I have a gentle aversion towards editors who include their own work in anthologies – too much like vanity publishing. Even leaving aside the blatant self-promotion, it steals space from writers who might otherwise benefit from being represented. For these reasons, I've declined to publish any of my own poetry in this book.

The changing nature of the island poet's role in society over the years has been interesting. Whereas the traditional island poet stayed at home and wrote formal verse for a localised audience, the contemporary island poet is likely to be a well-travelled, well-educated writer of free verse with a comparatively large (potential) audience. Modern technology has, in one sense, made writing easier than ever. The internet can facilitate, within seconds, research that would once have necessitated far greater expenditure of time and effort. Computers allow us to type and redraft with ease. We can explore with minimal effort the literary endeavours of fellow poets in other places.

Appreciation of tradition carries with it an awareness of the importance of adding to that tradition rather than emulating it, which constitutes a kind of theft from future readers. I have confidence that the islands will, in due course, give us a more diverse ethnic and linguistic spread of writers. I think we will see more prose efforts, and the reticence many islanders feel towards novel-writing shall fade. Technology will assert itself in the writer's life still further, and cross-genre collaborations and multi-media projects will proliferate.

Working on this book was a pleasure. It was a joy to re-read classic poems and a thrill to discover new ones, including previously unpublished works by established and emergent talents. I hope this anthology will help encourage poets and readers to continue creating and supporting work that is beyond material price. Scotland's island literature is ever evolving. May future editions strengthen accordingly.

Kevin MacNeil

EDWIN MUIR

Childhood

Long time he lay upon the sunny hill,
  To his father's house below securely bound.
Far off the silent, changing sound was still,
  With the black islands lying thick around.

He saw each separate height, each vaguer hue,
  Where the massed islands rolled in mist away,
And though all ran together in his view
  He knew that unseen straits between them lay.

Often he wondered what new shores were there.
  In thought he saw the still light on the sand,
The shallow water clear in tranquil air,
  And walked through it in joy from strand to strand.

Over the sound a ship so slow would pass
  That in the black hill's gloom it seemed to lie.
The evening sound was smooth like sunken glass,
  And time seemed finished ere the ship passed by.

Grey tiny rocks slept round him where he lay,
  Moveless as they, more still as evening came,
The grasses threw straight shadows far away,
  And from the house his mother called his name.

Houses

The far house shines so clear, it seems to come
   Towards me across the green estranging land.
The chimneys clustering watch; a tiny hum
   Fills the closed rooms; the mute walls listening stand.

When as a child I walked upon the earth,
   In burning inquisition, half afraid,
Too empty seemed the wide horizon's girth,
   But there were nooks with magic thick inlaid;

But most where in a house in one green place
   Doors opened wide to low voice of a stream,
Where through still-standing days I seemed to pace,
   As if the years were tarrying in a dream.

There was a line around on every side,
   And all within spoke to me and was home.
Beyond, the empty fields spread waste and wide,
   To the dark sea where ships cut white the foam.

How long, how long I pored on stone and tree,
   In happy inward dream day after day!
Slow lifting up my heavy head to see
   Tall men walk on the white roads far away,

And houses standing still in sun and rain,
   With dreamt-of rustlings filled from roof to floor, –
Then I would watch for hours to see again
   The folk go out and in about the door.

Now I can see once more, once more can feel
   That human magic on the stony earth.
See, through their struggling web of stone and steel,
   Those distant houses shine with grief and mirth!

The Northern Islands

In favoured summers
These islands have the sun all to themselves
And light a toy to play with, weeks on end.
The empty sky and waters are a shell
Endlessly turning, turning the wheel of light,
While the tranced waves run wavering up the sand.
The beasts sleep when they can, midnight or midday,
Slumbering on into unending brightness.
The green, green fields give too much, are too rank
With beautiful beasts for breeding or for slaughter.
The horses, glorious useless race, are leaving.
Have the old ways left with them, and the faith,
Lost in this dream too comfortable and goodly
To make room for a blessing? Where can it fall?
The old ways change in the turning, turning light,
Taking and giving life to life from life.

An Island Tale

She had endured so long a grief
That from her breast we saw it grow,
Branch, leaf and flower with such a grace
We wondered at the summer place
Which set that harvest there. But oh
The softly, softly yellowing leaf.

She was enclosed in quietness,
Where for lost love her tears were shed.
They stopped, and she was quite alone.
Being so poor, she was our own,
Her lack of all our precious bread.
She had no skill to offer less.

She turned into an island song
And died. They sing her ballad yet,
But all the simple verses tell
Is, Love and grief became her well.
Too well; for how can we forget
Her happy face when she was young?

The Swimmer's Death

He lay outstretched upon the sunny wave,
That turned and broke into eternity.
The light showed nothing but a glassy grave
Among the trackless tumuli of the sea.
Then over his buried brow and eyes and lips
From every side flocked in the homing ships.

HUGH MACDIARMID

Perfect

On the Western Seaboard of South Uist
(Los muertos abren los ojos a los que viven)

I found a pigeon's skull on the machair,
All the bones pure white and dry, and chalky,
But perfect,
Without a crack or a flaw anywhere

At the back, rising out of the beak,
Were twin domes like bubbles of thin bone,
Almost transparent, where the brain had been
That fixed the tilt of the wings.

FROM *Shetland Lyrics*

I

With the Herring Fishers

'I see herrin'.' – I hear the glad cry
And 'gainst the moon see ilka blue jowl
In turn as the fishermen haul on the nets
And sing: 'Come, shove in your heids and growl.'

'Soom on, bonnie herrin', soom on,' they shout,
Or 'Come in, O come in, and see me,'
'Come gie the auld man something to dae.
It'll be a braw change frae the sea.'

O it's ane o' the bonniest sichts in the warld
To watch the herrin' come walkin' on board
In the wee sma' 'oors o' a simmer's mornin'
As if o' their ain accord.

For this is the way that God sees life,
The haill jing-bang o's appearin'
Up owre frae the edge o' naethingness
– It's his happy cries I'm hearin'.

'Left, right – O come in and see me,'
Reid and yellow and black and white
Toddlin' up into Heaven thegither
At peep o' day frae the endless night.

'I see herrin',' I hear his glad cry,
And 'gainst the moon see his muckle blue jowl,
As he handles buoy-tow and bush-raip
Singin': 'Come, shove in your heids and growl!'

2

Deep-Sea Fishing

I suddenly saw I was wrang when I felt
That the gapin' mooths and gogglin' een
O' the fish were no' what we should expect
Frae a sea sae infinite and serene.

I kent I'd be equally wrang if I wished
My nice concern wi' its beauty to be
Shared by the fishermen wha's coarser lives
Seemed proof to a' that appealed to me.

Aye, and I kent their animal forms
And primitive minds, like fish frae the sea,
Cam' faur mair naturally oot o' the bland
Omnipotence o' God than a fribble like me.

3

Colla Firth in Winter

Nae mair wi' a bricht kerchief rowed roon her heid
Bonnie lass by bonnie lass eidently bends
Owre the lang row o' farlins doon the quayside
Wi' piles o' glitterin' herrin' at her quick finger ends.

There's a press o' craft roond the pierheid nae mair,
Sailin' boats, motor boats, drifters and a'
Wi' cran baskets swingin' and trollies kept ga'en
A' the 'oors o' the mornin' as hard's they can ca'.

I dodge oot and in o' the shadowy voes
Wi' nae fishermen to crack wi', nae lassies to tease.
There's naething to hear and naething to see
Save whiles a ferlie my ain spirit gi'es.

Why am *I* still here while a' else is awa'?
Why has time ta'en the lave and spared naething but me?
Is it freendship or juist the whim o' a foe?
Naething else can I miss wi' this riddle to ree!

5

Gruney

You say there's naething here
   But a bank o' snaw?
But the sun whiles shows in't
   Gleg een ana'.

I'll be like these white birds
   Sittin' facin' the ocean
Wi' here and there in their stillness
   Vigil's pin-point motion.

6

The Bonxie

I'll be the Bonxie, that noble scua,
That infects a' ither birds wi' its qualms.
In its presence even the eagle
Forbears to pounce on the lambs.

For it fechts wi' nocht less than itsel'
And prefers to encoonter great odds.
Guid-bye to mankind. Henceforth I'll engage
Only angels, archangels, devils and gods.

7

To a Sea Eagle

I used to walk on solid gr'und
Till it fell awa' frae my feet
And, left in the void, I'd instantly
To get accustomed wi't.

Watchin' your prood flight noo I feel
As a man may dae wi' a bairn,
For withoot ony show at a'
In deeper abysses I'm farin'.

Aye, withoot ony show at a',
Save whiles a sang I may sing
Gets in resonance wi' the sun
And ootshines't like a turnin' wing.

Shags' Nests

Shags build their slatternly nests
On a ledge o' a slot
In the rocky coast, where they're easily found
Frae below by a man in a boat.

But they canna be seen frae abune
– And in that remind me
Aince mair o' the death-bound spirits o' men
That, climbin', I've left behind me.

In the Shetland Islands

I am no further from the 'centre of things'
In the Shetlands here than in London, New York, or Tokio,
No further from 'the great warm heart of humanity',
Or the 'general good', no less 'central to human destiny',
Sitting alone here enjoying life's greatest good,
The pleasure of my own company,
Than if I were one with the crowds in the streets
In any of the great centres of population,
Or in a mile-long cinema queue, or a unit
In a two-hundred-thousand spectatorate
At Twickenham or Murrayfield or Ibrox
Or reading a selection of today's newspapers
Rather than Keller's *Probleme der englischen Sprache und Kultur*,
Or Heuser's *Die Kildare-Gedichte: die ältesten
mittel-englischen Denkmäler in anglo-irischer Überlieferung*,
Or Esposito's articles in *Hermathena*
On the Latin writers of mediaeval Ireland,
Or Curtis on *The Spoken Languages
Of Mediaeval Ireland*, or Heuser on the peculiar dialect

Of English spoken less than a hundred years ago
– Direct descendant of the language of the Kildare poems –
In the baronies of Forth and Bargy in County Wexford
And often (wrongly) described as a mainly Flemish speech.

The newspaper critic was talking rubbish, as usual,
When he made the shallow gibe, the fool reproach,
That in resuming his work in the Castle of Muzot
Rilke with all his insistence on *Bejahung*
'Could only praise life when protected from it.'

If personal participation were to be demanded,
Privacy forbidden, and any abstention
From any show of 'life' – from any activity
Most people indulge in – construed
As a flight from reality, an insulation from Life,
All but the most rudimentary forms of life,
All but the 'life' of the stupidest people,
Would speedily become impossible.
Rilke at Muzot or Duino was no more
'Protected from life' than any fool
At a street corner or in the House of Commons
Or in the columns of *The Scotsman*.
To be exclusively concerned with the highest forms of life
Is not to be less alive than 'normal' people.

TORMOD MACLEÒID

Raoir chunna mi

Raoir chunna mi, troimh dhual-chuailean
   Na gruagaich uasail mhàld',
A' ghealach ùr is crùb oirre,
   Tigh'nn cùl nan cnoc air fàth.

'N e h-aonrachd fhéin chuir sgoinn oirre
   Gu farchlais air ar luaidh,
I naomhachadh le h-òr-bhoillsgeadh
   An ceòl cridhe bh' oirnn mun cuairt?

Ailleanachd air m' eudail
   'S a crìdh air sgéith 'na sùil,
Iongnadh air a tlàth-bhilean
   'S ar gràdh 'na shàmhchair ciùil.

A Rìgh, ged dheadh gach bliadhna dhomh
   A shnìomh 'na linn 's 'na ré,
Bidh h-ìomhaigh chaoin 's a sèimhealachd
   'Na naomhachd shìor 'nam chré.

Bàgh Leumrabhaigh

Iùbhrach fo sheòl an òr-shruth na gealaich,
   Osann na mar' air an tràigh;
An oiteag bho thìr gu mìn tigh'nn thairis,
   Gu fann toirt fannadh don bhàt';
Aiteal á doimhne cuimhne m' earraich
   Fa m' chomhair am foghar mo là.

NORMAN MACLEOD

Last night I saw

Last night I saw, through the curly locks
    Of the modest gentle girl,
The new moon crouched stealthily,
    Peeping from behind the hills.

Was it loneliness that brought it
    To eavesdrop on our talk
As it sanctified with its aura
    The heart's music enfolding us?

How perfect is my darling
    With her heart on wing in her eye,
Wondrous are her gentle lips
    When our love is musical silence.

O King, should every year for me
    Be spun into era and age,
Her gentle face and softness
    Will still sanctify my clay.

Lemreway Bay

A boat under sail in the moon's golden path,
    Ocean's sigh upon strand;
The breeze from the land wafting gently across,
    Weakly propelling the craft;
A gleam from the deep is my memory of spring
    Recalled in the autumn of life.

(English versions by Ronald Black)

T. A. ROBERTSON ('VAGALAND')

Kwarna farna?*

A laar o Wast wind blaain
   Keeps doon da waarm ön;
I hear da Baas o Huxter,
   An hear da laverik's tön
   Ita da lift abön.

Da lochs, trowe bricht daals lyin,
   Spreads wide dir sheenin net;
Da simmermil is mirrlin
   By skerry, stack, an klett;
   Bit shön da sun will set.

You see noo, every saison,
   Run waas o barns an byres,
An rigs an cuts fast shangin
   Ta burra an ta mires,
   An little reek fae fires.

Eence Dale ta Brouster mustered
   A thoosand folk an mair
Ta dell, an draa da boats doon,
   An cast, an maa, an shair:
   Bit noo da laand is bare.

---

* Kwarna farna? Where are you going? (Old Norn)

Water-lilies

Whin da laeves an buds o da water-lilies
   Spread roond da loch dir dark-green frill
I took my tushkar be Lungawater
   An cöst a bank near Stoorbra Hill.

Da hill laek a kummelled boat wis lyin,
   Grown ower wi moss ida lang Jöne days,
An white apo white da water-lilies,
   Whin du cam dere wi me ta raise.

Da stack wis beelt an da coarn gaddered
   An dan I hed ta geng awa,
Bit I tink o da lilies aft wi langer,
   Noo everything is smoored in snaa.

I tink o dee be da oppen fire,
   As du sits an looks at da golden glöd
Laek gold ida cups o white water-lilies,
   Whaar I drank sweetness afore I göd.

SOMHAIRLE MACGILL-EAIN

An Roghainn

Choisich mi cuide ri mo thuigse
a-muigh ri taobh a' chuain;
bha sinn còmhla ach bha ise
a' fuireach tiotan bhuam.

An sin thionndaidh i ag ràdha:
a bheil e fìor gun cual
thu gu bheil do ghaol geal àlainn
a' pòsadh tràth Di-luain?

Bhac mi 'n cridhe bha 'g éirigh
'nam bhroilleach reubte luath
is thubhairt mi: tha mi cinnteach;
carson bu bhriag e bhuam?

Ciamar a smaoinichinn gun glacainn
an rionnag leugach òir,
gum beirinn oirre 's gun cuirinn i
gu ciallach 'na mo phòc?

Cha d' ghabh mise bàs croinn-ceusaidh
an éiginn chruaidh na Spàinn
is ciamar sin bhiodh dùil agam
ri aon duais ùir an dàin?

Cha do lean mi ach an t-slighe chrìon
bheag ìosal thioram thlàth,
is ciamar sin a choinnichinn
ri beithir-theine ghràidh?

Ach nan robh 'n roghainn rithist dhomh
's mi 'm sheasamh air an àird,
leumainn á nèamh no iutharna
le spiorad 's cridhe slàn.

SORLEY MACLEAN

The Choice

I walked with my reason
out beside the sea.
We were together but it was
keeping a little distance from me.

Then it turned saying:
is it true you heard
that your beautiful white love
is getting married early on Monday?

I checked the heart that was rising
in my torn swift breast
and I said: most likely;
why should I lie about it?

How should I think that I would grab
the radiant golden star,
that I would catch it and put it
prudently in my pocket?

I did not take a cross's death
in the hard extremity of Spain
and how then should I expect
the one new prize of fate?

I followed only a way
that was small, mean, low, dry, lukewarm,
and how then should I meet
the thunderbolt of love?

But if I had the choice again
and stood on that headland,
I would leap from heaven or hell
with a whole spirit and heart.

Ban-Ghàidheal

Am faca Tu i, Iùdhaich mhóir,
ri 'n abrar Aon Mhac Dhé?
Am fac' thu 'coltas air Do thriall
ri strì an fhìon-lios chéin?

An cuallach mhiosan air a druim,
fallus searbh air mala is gruaidh;
's a' mhias chreadha trom air cùl
a cinn chrùibte bhochd thruaigh.

Chan fhaca Tu i, Mhic an t-saoir,
ri 'n abrar Rìgh na Glòir,
a miosg nan cladach carrach siar,
fo fhallus cliabh a lòin.

An t-earrach seo agus seo chaidh
's gach fichead earrach bho 'n an tùs
tharruing ise 'n fheamainn fhuar
chum biadh a cloinne 's duais an tùir.

'S gach fichead foghar tha air triall
chaill i samhradh buidh nam blàth;
is threabh an dubh-chosnadh an clais
tarsuinn mìnead ghil a clàir.

Agus labhair T' eaglais chaomh
mu staid chaillte a h-anama thruaigh;
agus leag an cosnadh dian
a corp gu sàmhchair dhuibh an uaigh.

Is thriall a tìm mar shnighe dubh
a' drùdhadh tughaidh fàrdaich bochd;
mheal ise an dubh-chosnadh cruaidh;
is glas a cadal suain an nochd.

A Highland Woman

Hast Thou seen her, great Jew,
who art called the One Son of God?
Hast Thou seen on Thy way the like of her
labouring in the distant vineyard?

The load of fruits on her back,
a bitter sweat on brow and cheek,
and the clay basin heavy on the back
of her bent poor wretched head.

Thou hast not seen her, Son of the carpenter,
who art called the King of Glory,
among the rugged western shores
in the sweat of her food's creel.

This Spring and last Spring
and every twenty Springs from the beginning,
she has carried the cold seaweed
for her children's food and the castle's reward.

And every twenty Autumns gone
she has lost the golden summer of her bloom,
and the Black Labour has ploughed the furrow
across the white smoothness of her forehead.

And Thy gentle church has spoken
about the lost state of her miserable soul,
and the unremitting toil has lowered
her body to a black peace in a grave.

And her time has gone like a black sludge
seeping through the thatch of a poor dwelling:
the hard Black Labour was her inheritance;
grey is her sleep tonight.

Am Bàta Dubh

A bhàta dhuibh, a Ghreugaich choimhlionta,
cluas siùil, balg siùil làn is geal,
agus tu fhéin gu foirfeach ealanta,
sàmhach uallach gun ghiamh gun ghais;
do chùrsa réidh gun bhròn gun fhaireachadh;
cha b' iadsan luingis dhubha b' ealanta
a sheòl Odysseus a nall á Itaca
no Mac Mhic Ailein a nall á Uibhist,
cuid air muir fìon-dhorcha
's cuid air sàl uaine-ghlas.

An t-Eilean

Thug thu dhomh an cuibheas luachmhor
agus beagan mheanmnachd bhuadhan,
spàirn, cunnart agus aighear suilbhir
air mullaichean garbh' a' Chuilithinn,
agus fodham eilean leugach,
gaol mo chuideachd, mire 'n léirsinn,
an seachdnar is càch am Port-rìgh,
iomairt spioraid 's eanchainn; strì
chaman Sgitheanach air budha na h-aibhne,
mire chatha, comunn aoibhneach;
is oidhcheannan an Aodainn-Bhàin,
bòidhchead, òl, is annas bhàrd,
geurad, éisgeachd, éibhneas làn,
an aigne Sgitheanach aig a bàrr;
is oidhcheannan air ruighe Lìondail,
an t-Eilean mór 's a mheallan lìontach
'nan laighe sìthe anns a' chiaradh,
glaisneulach gu bristeadh iarmailt.

The Black Boat

Black boat, perfect Greek,
sail tack, sail belly full and white,
and you yourself complete in craft,
silent, spirited, flawless;
your course smooth, sorrowless, unfeeling;
they were no more skilled black ships
that Odysseus sailed over from Ithaca,
or Clanranald over from Uist,
those on a wine-dark sea,
those on a grey-green brine.

The Island

You gave me the valuable enough
and some mettlesome talent,
struggle, danger and pleasant high spirits
on the rugged tops of the Cuillin,
and under me a jewel-like island,
love of my people, delight of their eyes;
the Seven and the rest in Portree,
exercise of brain and spirit, strife
of Skye camans on the river bught,
battle-joy, joyous company;
and the nights of Edinbane,
beauty, drink and poets' novelties,
wit, satire, delight in full,
the Skye spirit at its height;
and nights on the slope of Lyndale,
the great Island with its many hills
lying in peace in the twilight,
grey-faced till the breaking of the sky.

O Eilein mhóir, Eilein mo ghaoil,
is iomadh oidhche dhiubh a shaoil
liom an cuan mór fhéin bhith luasgan
le do ghaol-sa air a bhuaireadh
is tu 'nad laighe air an fhairge,
eòin mhóir sgiamhaich na h-Albann,
do sgiathan àlainn air an lùbadh
mu Loch Bhràcadail ioma-chùilteach,
do sgiathan bòidheach ri muir sleuchdte
bho 'n Eist Fhiadhaich gu Aird Shléite,
do sgiathan aoibhneach air an sgaoileadh
mu Loch Shnigheasort 's mu 'n t-saoghal!

O Eilein mhóir, m' Eilein, mo chiall,
's iomadh oidhche shìn mi riamh
ri do thaobh-sa anns an t-suain ud
is ceò na camhanaich 'gad shuaineadh!
Is gràdhach liom gach bileag fraoich ort
bho Rubha Hùnais gu Loch Shlaopain,
agus gach bileag roid dhomh càirdeach
o Shròin Bhiornaill gus a' Ghàrsbheinn,
gach lochan, sruth is abhainn aoibhneach
o Ròmasdal gu Bràigh Aoineart,
agus ged a nochdainn Pàrras,
dé b' fhiach a ghealach-san gun Bhlàbheinn?

Eilein Mhóir, Eilein mo dheòin,
Eilein mo chridhe is mo leòin,
chan eil dùil gum faicear pàighte
strì is allaban a' Bhràighe,
is chan eil cinnt gum faicear fiachan
Martarach Ghleann-Dail 's iad dìolte;
chan eil dòchas ri do bhailtean
éirigh ard le gàire 's aiteas,
's chan eil fiughair ri do dhaoine
's Aimeireaga 's an Fhraing 'gam faotainn.

Mairg an t-sùil a chì air fairge
ian mór marbh na h-Albann.

O great Island, Island of my love,
many a night of them I fancied
the great ocean itself restless,
agitated with love of you
as you lay on the sea,
great beautiful bird of Scotland,
your supremely beautiful wings bent
about many-nooked Loch Bracadale,
your beautiful wings prostrate on the sea
from the Wild Stallion to the Aird of Sleat,
your joyous wings spread
about Loch Snizort and the world.

O great Island, my Island, my love,
many a night I lay stretched
by your side in that slumber
when the mist of twilight swathed you.
My love every leaflet of heather on you
from Rubha Hunish to Loch Slapin,
and every leaflet of bog-myrtle
from Stron Bhiornaill to the Garsven,
every tarn, stream and burn a joy
from Romisdale to Brae Eynort,
and even if I came in sight of Paradise,
what price its moon without Blaven?

Great Island, Island of my desire,
Island of my heart and wound,
it is not likely that the strife
and suffering of Braes will be seen requited
and it is not certain that the debts
of the Glendale Martyr will be seen made good;
there is no hope of your townships
rising high with gladness and laughter,
and your men are not expected
when America and France take them.

Pity the eye that sees on the ocean
the great dead bird of Scotland.

Coin is Madaidhean-allaidh

Thar na sìorruidheachd, thar a sneachda,
chì mi mo dhàin neo-dheachdte,
chì mi lorgan an spòg a' breacadh
gile shuaimhneach an t-sneachda:
calg air bhoile, teanga fala,
gadhair chaola 's madaidhean-allaidh
a' leum thar mullaichean nan gàrradh,
a' ruith fo sgàil nan craobhan fàsail,
a' gabhail cumhang nan caol-ghleann,
a' sireadh caisead nan gaoth-bheann;
an langan gallanach a' sianail
thar loman cruaidhe nan àm cianail,
an comhartaich bhiothbhuan na mo chluasan,
an deann-ruith a' gabhail mo bhuadhan:
réis nam madadh 's nan con iargalt
luath air tòrachd an fhiadhaich
troimh na coilltean gun fhiaradh,
thar mullaichean nam beann gun shiaradh;
coin chiùine caothaich na bàrdachd,
madaidhean air tòir na h-àilleachd,
àilleachd an anama 's an aodainn,
fiadh geal thar bheann is raointean,
fiadh do bhòidhche ciùine gaolaich,
fiadhach gun sgur gun fhaochadh.

Dogs and Wolves

Across eternity, across its snows,
I see my unwritten poems,
I see the spoor of their paws dappling
the untroubled whiteness of the snow:
bristles raging, bloody-tongued,
lean greyhounds and wolves
leaping over the tops of the dykes,
running under the shade of the trees of the wilderness,
taking the defile of narrow glens,
making for the steepness of windy mountains;
their baying yell shrieking
across the hard barenesses of the terrible times,
their everlasting barking in my ears,
their onrush seizing my mind:
career of wolves and eerie dogs
swift in pursuit of the quarry,
through the forests without veering,
over the mountain tops without sheering;
the mild mad dogs of poetry,
wolves in chase of beauty,
beauty of soul and face,
a white deer over hills and plains,
the deer of your gentle beloved beauty,
a hunt without halt, without respite.

Tràighean

Nan robh sinn an Talasgar air an tràigh
far a bheil am bial mór bàn
a' fosgladh eadar dà ghiall chruaidh,
Rubha nan Clach 's am Bioda Ruadh,
sheasainn-sa ri taobh na mara
ag ùrachadh gaoil 'nam anam
fhad 's a bhiodh an cuan a' lìonadh
camus Thalasgair gu sìorruidh:
sheasainn an siod air lom na tràghad
gu 'n cromadh Priseal a cheann àigich.

Agus nan robh sinn cuideachd
air traigh Chalgaraidh am Muile,
eadar Alba is Tiriodh,
eadar an saoghal 's a' bhiothbhuan,
dh'fhuirichinn an siod gu luan
a' tomhas gainmhich bruan air bhruan.
Agus an Uibhist air tràigh Hòmhstaidh
fa chomhair farsuingeachd na h-ònrachd,
dh'fheithinn-sa an siod gu sìorruidh
braon air bhraon an cuan a' sìoladh.

Agus nan robh mi air tràigh Mhùideart
còmhla riut, a nodhachd ùidhe,
chuirinn suas an cochur gaoil dhut
an cuan 's a' ghaineamh, bruan air bhraon dhiubh.
'S nan robh sinn air Mol Steinnseil Stamhain
's an fhairge neo-aoibhneach a' tarruing
nan ulbhag is 'gan tilgeil tharainn,
thogainn-sa am balla daingeann
roimh shìorruidheachd choimhich 's i framhach.

Shores

If we were in Talisker on the shore
where the great white mouth
opens between two hard jaws,
Rubha nan Clach and the Bioda Ruadh,
I would stand beside the sea
renewing love in my spirit
while the ocean was filling
Talisker bay forever:
I would stand there on the bareness of the shore
until Prishal bowed his stallion head.

And if we were together
on Calgary shore in Mull,
between Scotland and Tiree,
between the world and eternity,
I would stay there till doom
measuring sand, grain by grain.
And in Uist, on the shore of Homhsta
in presence of that wide solitude,
I would wait there forever
for the sea draining drop by drop.

And if I were on the shore of Moidart
with you, for whom my care is new,
I would put up in a synthesis of love for you
the ocean and the sand, drop and grain.
And if we were on Mol Stenscholl Staffin
when the unhappy surging sea dragged
the boulders and threw them over us,
I would build the rampart wall
against an alien eternity grinding (its teeth).

Am Mùr Gorm

Mur b' e thusa bhiodh an Cuilithionn
'na mhùr eagarra gorm
a' crioslachadh le bhalla-crìche
na tha 'nam chridhe borb.

Mur b' e thusa bhiodh a' ghaineamh
tha 'n Talasgar dùmhail geal
'na clàr biothbhuan do mo dhùilean,
air nach tilleadh an rùn-ghath.

'S mur b' e thusa bhiodh na cuantan
'nan luasgan is 'nan tàmh
a' togail càir mo bhuadhan,
'ga cur air suaimhneas àrd.

'S bhiodh am monadh donn riabhach
agus mo chiall co-shìnt' –
ach chuir thusa orra riaghladh
os cionn mo phianaidh fhìn.

Agus air creachainn chéin fhàsmhoir
chinn blàthmhor Craobh nan Teud,
'na meangach duillich t' aodann,
mo chiall is aogas réil.

The Blue Rampart

But for you the Cuillin would be
an exact and serrated blue rampart
girdling with its march-wall
all that is in my fierce heart.

But for you the sand
that is in Talisker compact and white
would be a measureless plain to my expectations
and on it the spear desire would not turn back.

But for you the oceans
in their unrest and their repose
would raise the wave-crests of my mind
and settle them on a high serenity.

And the brown brindled moorland
and my reason would co-extend –
but you imposed on them an edict
above my own pain.

And on a distant luxuriant summit
there blossomed the Tree of Strings,
among its leafy branches your face,
my reason and the likeness of a star.

Reothairt

Uair is uair agus mi briste
thig mo smuain ort is tu òg,
is lìonaidh an cuan do-thuigsinn
le làn-mara 's mìle seòl.

Falaichear cladach na trioblaid
le bhodhannan is tiùrr a' bhròin
is buailidh an tonn gun bhristeadh
mu m' chasan le suathadh sròil.

Ciamar nach do mhair an reothairt
bu bhuidhe dhomh na do na h-eòin,
agus a chaill mi a cobhair
's i tràghadh boinn' air bhoinne bròin?

Spring Tide

Again and again when I am broken
my thought comes on you when you were young,
and the incomprehensible ocean fills
with floodtide and a thousand sails.

The shore of trouble is hidden
with its reefs and the wrack of grief,
and the unbreaking wave strikes
about my feet with a silken rubbing.

How did the springtide not last,
the springtide more golden to me than to the birds,
and how did I lose its succour,
ebbing drop by drop of grief?

Hallaig

'Tha tìm, am fiadh, an coille Hallaig'

Tha bùird is tàirnean air an uinneig
troimh 'm faca mi an Aird an Iar
's tha mo ghaol aig Allt Hallaig
'na craoibh beithe, 's bha i riamh

eadar an t–Inbhir 's Poll a' Bhainne,
thall 's a bhos mu Bhaile-Chùirn:
tha i 'na beithe, 'na calltuinn,
'na caorunn dhìreach sheang ùir.

Ann an Screapadal mo chinnidh,
far robh Tarmad 's Eachann Mór,
tha 'n nigheanan 's am mic 'nan coille
a' gabhail suas ri taobh an lóin.

Uaibhreach a nochd na coilich ghiuthais
a' gairm air mullach Cnoc an Rà,
dìreach an druim ris a' ghealaich –
chan iadsan coille mo ghràidh.

Fuirichidh mi ris a' bheithe
gus an tig i mach an Càrn,
gus am bi am bearradh uile
o Bheinn na Lice f' a sgàil.

Mura tig 's ann theàrnas mi a Hallaig,
a dh'ionnsaigh sàbaid nam marbh,
far a bheil an sluagh a' tathaich,
gach aon ghinealach a dh'fhalbh.

Tha iad fhathast ann a Hallaig,
Clann Ghill-Eain 's Clann MhicLeòid,
na bh' ann ri linn Mhic Ghille Chaluim:
chunnacas na mairbh beò.

Hallaig

'Time, the deer, is in the wood of Hallaig'

The window is nailed and boarded
through which I saw the West
and my love is at the Burn of Hallaig,
a birch tree, and she has always been

between Inver and Milk Hollow,
here and there about Baile-chuirn:
she is a birch, a hazel,
a straight, slender young rowan.

In Screapadal of my people,
where Norman and Big Hector were,
their daughters and their sons are a wood
going up beside the stream.

Proud tonight the pine cocks
crowing on the top of Cnoc an Ra,
straight their backs in the moonlight –
they are not the wood I love.

I will wait for the birch wood
until it comes up by the cairn,
until the whole ridge from Beinn na Lice
will be under its shade.

If it does not, I will go down to Hallaig,
to the Sabbath of the dead,
where the people are frequenting,
every single generation gone.

They are still in Hallaig,
MacLeans and MacLeods,
all who were there in the time of Mac Gille Chaluim:
the dead have been seen alive.

Na fir 'nan laighe air an lèanaig
aig ceann gach taighe a bh' ann,
na h-igheanan 'nan coille bheithe,
dìreach an druim, crom an ceann.

Eadar an Leac is na Feàrnaibh
tha 'n rathad mór fo chóinnich chiùin,
's na h-igheanan 'nam badan sàmhach
a' dol a Chlachan mar o thùs.

Agus a' tilleadh às a' Chlachan,
à Suidhisnis 's à tìr nam beò;
a chuile té òg uallach,
gun bhristeadh cridhe an sgeòil.

O Allt na Feàrnaibh gus an fhaoilinn
tha soilleir an dìomhaireachd nam beann
chan eil ach coimhthional nan nighean
a' cumail na coiseachd gun cheann.

A' tilleadh a Hallaig anns an fheasgar,
anns a' chamhanaich bhalbh bheò,
a' lìonadh nan leathadan casa,
an gàireachdaich 'nam chluais 'na ceò,

's am bòidhche 'na sgleò air mo chridhe
mun tig an ciaradh air na caoil,
's nuair theàrnas grian air cùl Dhùn Cana
thig peileir dian à gunna Ghaoil;

's buailear am fiadh a tha 'na thuaineal
a' snòtach nan làraichean feòir;
thig reothadh air a shùil sa choille:
chan fhaighear lorg air fhuil ri in' bheò.

The men lying on the green
at the end of every house that was,
the girls a wood of birches,
straight their backs, bent their heads.

Between the Leac and Fearns
the road is under mild moss
and the girls in silent bands
go to Clachan as in the beginning,

and return from Clachan,
from Suisnish and the land of the living;
each one young and light-stepping,
without the heartbreak of the tale.

From the Burn of Fearns to the raised beach
that is clear in the mystery of the hills,
there is only the congregation of the girls
keeping up the endless walk,

coming back to Hallaig in the evening,
in the dumb living twilight,
filling the steep slopes,
their laughter a mist in my ears,

and their beauty a film on my heart
before the dimness comes on the kyles,
and when the sun goes down behind Dun Cana
a vehement bullet will come from the gun of Love;

and will strike the deer that goes dizzily,
sniffing at the grass-grown ruined homes;
his eye will freeze in the wood,
his blood will not be traced while I live.

Bàs Baile

Chaidh am fuadach gu cùl a' chladaich
is shlaod iad bith-beò á talamh creagach.
Ged bha muir fiadhaich, bha tràigh fialaidh
is dh'fhàs na balaich mór.

An-dràst' 's a-rithist
thigeadh cairteal tombac'
is leth-bhotal uisge-bheath'
agus gu 'm màthair bocsa
le aodach aost' mì-fhreagarrach
bho Chomann còir nam Ban Uasal.

Sgrìobh i litir,
toirt taing am Beurla bhriste,
gu mnathan a' bhaile mhóir.
Aig céilidh an Dùn Éideann
chaidh a leughadh 's rinn iad fanaid.
'S thuirt mnathan uaisle le gàire,
Cuiridh sinn thuic' bocsa
seann aodaich eile
agus gheibh sinn litir éibhinn
le tuilleadh dibhearsain.

Is ràinig am bocsa sàbhailt'
baile cùl-a'-chladaich:
gùn is seacaid saighdeir,
briogais is còta ministeir,
b'e rud e air son cur bhuntàt'!
Dh'fhalbh litir am Beurla bhriste
is rinn uaislean a' bhaile mhóir gàir'.

REV. JOHN MACLEOD

The Death of a Township

They were cleared to the back of the shore
to eke a living out of rocky land.
Though sea was savage, ebb was generous
and the boys grew big.

Now and again
a quarter of tobacco would come
and a half-bottle of whisky
and to their mother a box
of old unsuitable clothes
from the dear Ladies' Association.

She wrote a letter,
sending thanks in broken English
to the ladies of the city.
At a ceilidh in Edinburgh
it was read and they mocked.
And ladies said laughing,
We'll send her another
box of old clothes
and get a comical letter
with more entertainment.

And the box reached in safety
the back-of-the-shore township:
a gown and a soldier's tunic,
a minister's trousers and jacket,
just the thing for planting potatoes!
Off went a letter in broken English
and the city gentry laughed.

Thàinig Bìoball teaghlaich Gàidhlig
is searmoinean Spurgeon le litir dhiadhaidh
ag iarraidh orr' bhith riaraicht'
leis na nithean bha làthair.

Mo ghràdh-sa òigridh ar là
'nam fiasaig dhùint' bho chluais gu cluais.
Mun d'ràinig na balaich againn aois fiasaig
no aois smaoineachaidh
dh'éigh iad Cogadh
is chaidh am marbhadh anns an Fhraing.
Bha 'm murt ud laghail.

A' chuid dhiubh a thàrr ás,
fhuair an fhairge iad a' tilleadh dhachaigh
agus dh'fhàg i na cuirp air an tràigh
's b'e marbh-phaisg fhuar an fheamainn.

A' chuid a thill leòinte 's beò,
cha robh gam feitheamh ach geallaidhean briste –
bàtaichean is lìn a' breothadh,
iasg gu leòr sa chuan gun comas thoirt ás.
Bhuain iad mòine, chuir iad buntàta
is chaidh le crodh gu àirigh
is dh'fhàs cnàmhan briste làidir.

Cur seachad oidhche gheamhraidh
chaidh na balaich chun an taigh-sgoile
a dh'fhaicinn dealbhan mu Chanada
le 'magic lantern'. Dé 'n cron a bh' ann?
Is chunnaic iad crodh am feur gu 'n cluasan,
caileag bhòidheach 's a h-uchd air geat
le fiamh a' ghàir' is sràbh 'na bial,
is chaidh iad dhachaigh 'g ràdh, Tha sinne falbh.
Thuirt a' chlann-nighean, Thà is sinne.

There came a Gaelic family Bible
and Spurgeon's sermons with a pious letter
asking them to be content
with what they had.

How I love the modern youngsters
enclosed in beards from ear to ear.
Before our lads reached beard-growing age
or were old enough to think
War was declared
and they were killed in France.
That murder was lawful.

Those of them who survived,
the sea got them on their way home
and left the bodies on the beach
and the seaweed was a cold shroud.

Those who returned wounded and alive,
nothing awaited them but broken promises –
boats and nets rotting,
fish aplenty in the sea without the means to take it out.
They cut peats, planted potatoes
and went with cattle to shieling
and broken bones grew strong.

By way of passing a winter's night
the lads went to the schoolhouse
to see pictures about Canada
with a 'magic lantern'. What was the harm?
And they saw cows up to their ears in grass,
a lovely girl leaning on a gate
smiling with a straw in her mouth,
and they went home saying, We're off.
The girls said, So are we.

Rev. John MacLeod 39

Lìon gach màthair ciste le aodach blàth
airson talamh fuar, is Bìoball anns gach seotal.
An oidhch' a dh'fhalbh iad
dhìrich sinn an cnoc a b' àirde
is shuidh sinn gun fhacal, sàmhach,
gus an deach ás ar sealladh
solas crann–àrd a' *Mharloch*.
Sin thòisich glaodh taigh–fhaireadh
aig tiodhlacadh daoine beò.
An oidhch' ud bhàsaich am bail' againn.

Each mother filled a kist with warm clothes
for a cold land, with a Bible in each shottle.
The night they left
we climbed the highest hill
and sat wordless, silent,
till the *Marloch*'s mainmast light
disappeared from our sight.
Then the wake-house cry arose
for the burial of the living.
That night our township died.

(English version by Ronald Black)

WILLIAM J. TAIT

Fat Marget's Ballade
(Villon)

If my weel-willied dame I serve an love,
Man I be held a toetak or a nyaff?
In her is every bliss your hert can muv,
An, feth, nor sword nor shield ta fend ye aff;
Fur, whin da men come, I rin furt an skaff
A pint or twa, no toed at laek a foel.
I bring dem maet ta aet an watter coel,
An if dey pey weel, tell dem: 'Sae be dat!
Come ye again whin niest ye're arg ta roel,
Here i dis hoorhoose whaar we had wis at.'

Bit, later on, dir herns an wallawa,
Whin Marget comes to bed ithoot a plack:
I canna lyeuk at her, her neck I'd traa;
Her cotts, her slug, her buckled belt I tak
An swear A'll roup da lot ta get my wack.
Wi haands on hips, dis Antichrist roars oot
An swears by Jesus on da Cross at cloot
Or plag I sanna. Dan I nam a slat
An wraet a bloedy answer on her snoot,
Here i dis hoorhoose whaar we had wis at.

Dan we mak pace; she slips a monstrous fart.
(Shoe's ey as blaan-up as a bloed-swalled bug.)
Laachin, shoe lays her hand on me, an: 'Start!
Vite! Vite!' she says, an gies my prick a nug . . .
Syne, baith daid drunk, we sleep as soond's a clug.
Bit, whin shoe waakens an still feels da yuck,
Shoe climms on tap, fur faer her seed wants muck;
I gron below, as ony plank pressed flat.
Wi sic bed-wark, shoe's laid me fair in bruck,
Here i dis hoorhoose whaar we had wis at.

Snaa, hail, or blaa, I hae my bite o meat.
Sae be's A'm bitched, da bitch is still in haet.
Wha's wirt da maest? We baith geng da wan gaet.
Tane wards da tidder: da cat's as ill's da rat.
As we laek shaarn, shite shaests wis shoen an late.
We skail fae honour, an hit's joest as blate,
Here i dis hoorhoose whaar we had wis at.

The Gift (1949)

From the bare rock sprang the fabulous tree
Full-grown, and jewelled all the air with birds
And birdsong, blossom, leaf-nets lantern-lit
With glowing fruit. Charmed figures stood
We two within its cage of falling melody,
Nor knew the casual stone-fallen seed
Had crevice found and flourished, till deciduous day
Died and night found us each alone
Beneath the barren bird-denuded boughs.

But as each miracle of mutual day restored
The prime and winter's solstice was each single night,
Though still the calendar records but one brief spring,
I sit in this day's autumn, plunge my hands,
Arms elbow-deep, in leaves, in memories,
Releasing buried fragrance like the song of birds.

But someday, when aeon-years have laid their lodes
Of leafmould, when all seasons of this spring have fused
In time's hard crystal, then that single gem
From a dark shaft of memory I shall mine,
Release, not perfume, but prisoned fire to gild
This gift, your own, I give the world and you.

GEORGE MACKAY BROWN

Hamnavoe

My father passed with his penny letters
Through closes opening and shutting like legends
   When barbarous with gulls
   Hamnavoe's morning broke

On the salt and tar steps. Herring boats,
Puffing red sails, the tillers
   Of cold horizons, leaned
   Down the gull-gaunt tide

And threw dark nets on sudden silver harvests.
A stallion at the sweet fountain
   Dredged water, and touched
   Fire from steel-kissed cobbles.

Hard on noon four bearded merchants
Past the pipe-spitting pier-head strolled,
   Holy with greed, chanting
   Their slow grave jargon.

A tinker keened like a tartan gull
At cuithe-hung doors. A crofter lass
   Trudged through the lavish dung
   In a dream of cornstalks and milk.

Blessings and soup plates circled. Euclidian light
Ruled the town in segments blue and gray.
   The school bell yawned and lisped
   Down ignorant closes.

In 'The Arctic Whaler' three blue elbows fell,
Regular as waves, from beards spumy with porter,
    Till the amber day ebbed out
    To its black dregs.

The boats drove furrows homeward, like ploughmen
In blizzards of gulls. Gaelic fisher girls
    Flashed knife and dirge
    Over drifts of herring,

And boys with penny wands lured gleams
From the tangled veins of the flood. Houses went blind
    Up one steep close, for a
    Grief by the shrouded nets.

The kirk, in a gale of psalms, went heaving through
A tumult of roofs, freighted for heaven. And lovers
    Unblessed by steeples, lay under
    The buttered bannock of the moon.

He quenched his lantern, leaving the last door.
Because of his gay poverty that kept
    My seapink innocence
    From the worm and black wind;

And because, under equality's sun,
All things wear now to a common soiling,
    In the fire of images
    Gladly I put my hand
    To save that day for him.

The Old Women

Go sad or sweet or riotous with beer
Past the old women gossiping by the hour,
They'll fix on you from every close and pier
An acid look to make your veins run sour.

'No help,' they say, 'his grandfather that's dead
Was troubled with the same dry-throated curse,
And many a night he made the ditch his bed.
This blood comes welling from the same cracked source.'

On every kind of merriment they frown.
But I have known a gray-eyed sober boy
Sail to the lobsters in a storm, and drown.
Over his body dripping on the stones
Those same old hags would weave into their moans
An undersong of terrible holy joy.

Hamnavoe Market

They drove to the Market with ringing pockets.

Folster found a girl
Who put wounds on his face and throat,
Small and diagonal, like red doves.

Johnston stood beside the barrel.
All day he stood there.
He woke in a ditch, his mouth full of ashes.

Grieve bought a balloon and a goldfish.
He swung through the air.
He fired shotguns, rolled pennies, ate sweet fog from a stick.

Heddle was at the Market also.
I know nothing of his activities.
He is and always was a quiet man.

Garson fought three rounds with a negro boxer,
And received thirty shillings,
Much applause, and an eye loaded with thunder.

Where did they find Flett?
They found him in a brazen circle,
All flame and blood, a new Salvationist.

A gypsy saw in the hand of Halcro
Great strolling herds, harvests, a proud woman.
He wintered in the poorhouse.

They drove home from the Market under the stars
Except for Johnston
Who lay in a ditch, his mouth full of dying fires.

Old Fisherman with Guitar

A formal exercise for withered fingers.
   The head is bent,
      The eyes half closed, the tune
Lingers
      And beats, a gentle wing the west had thrown
   Against his breakwater wall with salt savage lament.
So fierce and sweet the song on the plucked string,
   Know now for truth
      Those hands have cut from the net
The strong
      Crab-eaten corpse of Jock washed from a boat
   One old winter, and gathered the mouth of Thora to his mouth.

Beachcomber

Monday I found a boot –
Rust and salt leather.
I gave it back to the sea, to dance in.

Tuesday a spar of timber worth thirty bob.
Next winter
It will be a chair, a coffin, a bed.

Wednesday a half can of Swedish spirits.
I tilted my head.
The shore was cold with mermaids and angels.

Thursday I got nothing, seaweed,
A whale bone,
Wet feet and a loud cough.

Friday I held a seaman's skull,
Sand spilling from it
The way time is told on kirkyard stones.

Saturday a barrel of sodden oranges.
A Spanish ship
Was wrecked last month at The Kame.

Sunday, for fear of the elders,
I sit on my bum.
What's heaven? A sea chest with a thousand gold coins.

Winter: An Island Boy

A snowflake
Came like a white butterfly on his nose.
The boy whose mouth had been filled with harp-songs,
The shepherd king
Gave, on the third step, his purest cry.
   At the root of the Tree of Man, an urn
   With dust of apple-blossom

Joseph, harvest-dreamer, counsellor of pharaohs
Stood on the fourth step.
He blessed the lingering Bread of Life.

He who had wrestled with an angel,
The third of the chosen,
Hailed the King of Angels on the fifth step.

Abel with his flute and fleeces
Who bore the first wound
Came to the sixth step with his pastorals.

On the seventh step down
The tall primal dust
Turned with a cry from digging and delving.

   Tomorrow the Son of Man will walk in a garden
   Through drifts of apple-blossom.

Peat Cutting

And we left our beds in the dark
And we drove a cart to the hill
And we buried the jar of ale in the bog
And our small blades glittered in the dayspring
And we tore dark squares, thick pages
From the Book of Fire
And we spread them wet on the heather
And horseflies, poisonous hooks,
Stuck in our arms
And we laid off our coats
And our blades sank deep into water
And the lord of the bog, the kestrel
Paced round the sun
And at noon we leaned on our tuskars
– The cold unburied jar
Touched, like a girl, a circle of burning mouths
And the boy found a wild bees' comb
And his mouth was a sudden brightness
And the kestrel fell
And a lark flashed a needle across the west
And we spread a thousand peats
Between one summer star
And the black chaos of fire at the earth's centre.

RUARAIDH MACTHÒMAIS

An Loch a Tuath

Tha 'n iarmailt ciùin, 's an Loch a Tuath
'na laighe suaint fo bhrat na h-oidhch',
's cha ghlac mo bhreithneachadh a chaoidh
ged shiùbhladh e air iteig luath,

Cion-fàth an aoibhneis a tha falbh
mar airgead-beò air leac mo smuain,
no cobhar bàn air clàr a' chuain,
no soillseadh reuil san anmoch bhalbh.

Tha Mirean nan Rionnag 'nam Chuimhne

Tha mirean nan rionnag 'nam chuimhne
an oidhche ud – is fhada bhuaith 'n dràsd –
a sheas mi, 'nam ghille, gad fheitheamh,
is dlùth-bhrat den t-sneachd air a' bhlàr
is na craobhan fo bhlàth,
geug bho gheug fo gheal-eallach an t-sneachda;
fuaim an uillt, tha e nochd ann am chlaigeann,
gun dòigh agam idir air seachnadh,
's mo chuimhne gun uachdar gun aigeann,
an oidhche ud a gheall mi dhut gràdh.

Cha b'e fuarad do bhilean no tosdachd do chridhe
thog m'aighear gu mireadh san àm,
ach an leum bha nad chuisle
's mo phògan gad ruigheachd,
's an leus bha nad shùilean
ged dh'fhàg e mis dall;

DERICK THOMSON

The North Loch (Broad Bay)

The sky is calm, and the North Loch
lies sleeping under the night's cloak,
and my conscious understanding can never grasp,
though it were to speed on a swift wing,

The cause of the joy that flows
like quicksilver on the stone of my thought,
or like white foam on the sea's plain,
or star shining in the still evening.

I Recall the Twinkling of the Stars

I recall the twinkling of the stars
that night – a long time ago –
I stood, a lad, waiting for you,
a close covering of snow on the ground
and the trees in bloom,
branch after branch covered in white snow;
the sound of the burn is in my head tonight,
since I have no way of avoiding –
my memory lacking surface or sea-floor –
that night I promised love to you.

It was not your lips' coldness nor your heart's stillness
that made my joy lightsome then,
but your pulse's beat
as my kisses reached you,
and the light in your eyes
though it left me blind;

thill thugam an rionnag,
is sneachd a' bhòn-uiridh,
am beadradh 's an ruithleum a bha aig an allt,
ged a tha mi gun dùil 'am
gu bheil ràith anns a' chùnntas
bheir thugam an sùgradh
's am mùirn a th'air chall.

Hè mandu, 's truagh nach falbhadh,
hè mandu, siud bho m' chuimhne,
hè mandu, sruthadh aiteamh,
hao ri oro, dhen a' chraoibh sin.

Thàinig mi 'n rathad an deireadh an earraich,
na craobhan fo mheangain 's an duilleach ri fàs,
's an tè a bha mar rium bha ise gam fharraid,
'Am faca tu ionad nas bòidhche na 'n t-àit-s'?'
'S ged a rinn mise gàir
agus còmhradh is moladh is samhla an t-sonais,
bha grodas an donais 'nam chridhe ga chnàmh,
's cha chuimhne leam eun bha sa' choill ud a' seinn,
is tha torman an uillt air dol bàs.

the star returned to me,
the snow of two years ago,
the sport and rush of the burn,
though I do not expect
that there's a season in the calendar
will bring me the joy
and the love that is lost.

Hè mandu, if only, if only,
hè mandu, I could forget,
hè mandu, thaw's dripping,
hao ri oro, from that tree.

I came that way at the end of spring,
the trees a mass of twigs, the leaves growing,
and the one who was with me kept saying to me
'Have you ever seen a lovelier place?'
and though I laughed,
and talked and praised, and seemed happy,
the canker of unhappiness was in my heart, consuming it,
and I do not recall a bird singing in that wood,
and the purling of the burn has gone dead.

Fàgail Leòdhais, 1949

Ghluais i air sgèith bhàrr na machrach,
a sgiathan liath-ghlas gan rèiteach,
's a' ghaoth ga togail 's ga leagail,
Tràigh Thuilm dol nas lugha
's a' Chearc dol 'na h-isean,
is chunnaic mi, mach bhon a Rubha,
dà dhruim Eilean Phabail sa' chuan,
am fonn ciar ann an sloistreadh na fairge,
ceò is smonmhar an uisge,
sgòthan dùmhail gan druideadh
mu eilean mo bhreith agus m'àraich.

Marcan-sìne mu chladaichean Leòdhais –
cha d'fhàg siud an cianalas orm-sa,
ged is iomadach snaidhm tha gam cheangal,
's 'se 'n fheadhainn a bhris mi as doirbh' dhomh.
An Cuan Sgìth steach gu cladach a' Bhràighe,
's chan iarrainn-sa falbh ás na fuireach,
chan iarrainn-sa fuireach na falbh ás,
ach ghiùlain an tràigh dheth mi 'n uiridh.

Thog i a sròn chun na sgòthan
's an ceathach ga cuairteach;
fuar, fann mar a chunnaic mi uair e
air mullach Beinn Labhar,
'na stiallagan fuadain
's 'na chuairteagan badach,
sìor dhùmhlachadh 's sìor dhol an gealad,
is dhìrich sinn mach ás a' gheamhradh
gu ruige na gile,
ag iarraidh na grèine,
is rèitich i druim fo a gathan.

Leaving Lewis, 1949

The plane took off from the machair,
adjusting its light-grey wings,
the wind lifting it and letting it drop,
Holm Beach growing smaller,
Hen Rock becoming a chicken,
and I saw, off Point,
the two ridges of Bayble Island in the sea,
the dark land lashed by foam,
mist and swirling rain,
dense clouds closing
round the island of my birth and rearing.

Spindthrift round Lewis shores –
that did not make me nostalgic,
though many knots bind me,
and the ones I broke are the hardest.
The Minch flowing in to the Bràighe shore,
and I would not wish to go or stay,
I would not wish to stay or go,
but the tide carried me off last year.

She lifted her nose to the clouds,
the mist surrounding her;
cold, faint as I once saw it
on the summit of Lawers,
in stray streaks
and eddying clumps,
steadily thickening and growing whiter,
and we rose out of winter
into brightness,
seeking the sun,
and she found an even keel in its rays.

Nan ruigeadh m'inntinn-sa sàmhchar
le bhith sìor dhol an àirde,
's nan lorgadh i rèite
fo ghathan na grèine,
dh'fhàgainn-s' a' mhachair gu sùnndach
is chuirinn am Bràigh air mo chùlaibh,
is dhèanainn-sa dìreadh gun mhùgaich
troimh dhùmhlachd nan neòil,
ach O!, tha mo chridhe ro chorrach
's an iarmailt tuilleadh is molach,
chan amais mi idir air solas
nach caill mi an aithghearr sa' cheò,
chan fhaic mi fodham mar shneachda
caitean nan neòil is na h-eachdraidh,
's cha ghluais m'inntinn gu beachdaidh
air eagal sluic-adhair a' bhròin.

'S ma ruigeas mo dhùthaich-sa slànachd
cha seachainn i dànachd,
's cha chaill i a nàir'
airson gealtachd is crìonachd a dòigh,
ach cuireas i sròn ris a' gharbhlaich,
's ri crìdh na droch-aimsir,
ag èirigh air sgiathan neo-chearbach
a-mach ás a' cheò,
gun chaoidh airson nithean a chailleadh,
gun mheatachd ri aghaidh a' ghaillinn,
gun chiamalas tlàth air a h-aire,
le misneach nach dìobair fo bhròn,
's ged a chailleadh i 'n rubha
le braise 's le àirde a siubhail,
gun coisinn i fiughair
na grèine air mullach nan sgòth.

If my mind could find peace
by steadily climbing,
and find steadiness
under the sun's rays,
I would leave the machair cheerfully
and put the Bràighe behind me,
climbing without moping
through the dense clouds,
but O, my heart is unsteady
and the sky too stormy,
I cannot find a light
that I do not quickly lose in the mist,
I do not see below me like snow
the map of cloud and history,
and my mind does not move incisively
for fear of sorrow's air-pockets.

And if my country attains wholeness
it will not shun boldness,
it will not lose its shame
for the cowardliness and barren wisdom of its ways,
but will turn its nose to the heights,
and the heart of the storm,
rising on confident wings
out of the mist,
not mourning what is lost,
unafraid in the face of the storm,
with no soft nostalgia,
with courage that does not fail through sorrow,
and though it should lose sight of the point
with the speed and height of its thrust,
it will win the hope
of the sun above the clouds.

Pabail

Air iomall an talamh-àitich, eadar dhà sholas,
tha a' churracag a' ruith 's a' stad, 's a' ruith 's a' stad,
is cobhar bàn a broillich, mar rionnag an fheasgair,
ga lorg 's ga chall aig mo shùilean,
is tùis an t-samhraidh
ga lorg 's ga chall aig mo chuinnlean,
is fras-mhullach tonn an t-sonais
ga lorg 's ga chall aig mo chuimhne.

Bàgh Phabail fodham, is baile Phabail air fàire,
sluaisreadh sìorraidh a' chuain, a lorg 's a shireadh
eadar clachan a' mhuil 's an eag nan sgeir,
is fo ghainmhich a' gheodha,
gluasad bithbhuan a' bhaile, am bàs 's an ùrtan,
an ùrnaigh 's an t-suirghe, is mìle cridhe
ag at 's a' seacadh, is ann an seo
tha a' churracag a' ruith 's a' stad, 's a' ruith 's a' stad.

Bayble

On the edge of the arable land, between two
lights, the plover runs and stops, and runs and
stops, the white foam of its breast like the star of
evening, discovered and lost in my looking, and
the fragrance of summer, discovered and lost by
my nostrils, and the topmost grains of the wave of
content, discovered and lost by my memory.

Bayble Bay below me, and the village on the
skyline, the eternal action of the ocean, its seeking
and searching between the pebble stones and in
the rock crannies, and under the sand of the
cove; the everlasting movement of the village,
death and christening, praying and courting, and
a thousand hearts swelling and sinking, and here,
the plover runs and stops, and runs and stops.

Làraichean

Tha làraichean thaighean shìos air an sgaoiltich,
's na feannagan bàna 'nan cadal
an achlais na tràghad,
's na h-eathraichean mòra ri grodadh
ri grèidheadh na grèine.
Air là samhraidh, o chionn leth-cheud blianna
thug am baile ceum air ais, 's a-nis,
tha 'n tobhta stòlda, feurach
air greimeachadh le freumhaich
's an tughadh air seacadh
's tha na feannagan fada bhon tràigh
a' tuiteam 'nan cadal,
's tha an samhradh gu bhith againn.

Tha an t-seann bhean a dh'innis an uiridh dhomh
eachdraidh nan taighean-saillidh,
is eachdraidh a h-òige fhèin,
is eachdraidh a' bhòn-dè sa' bhaile,
'na suidhe ri taobh na cagailt,
is am feasgar am fagas,
is an samhradh gu bhith againn,
is an geamhradh gu bhith againn.

Tha an t-seann bhean a dh'innis an uiridh dhomh
beagan de dh'eachdraidh a' bhaile
a' cnuasachd làithean an earraich,
's a' bualadh a' choirc anns an t-sabhal,
's ga bhleith leis a' bhrà a ghlèidh i,
's a' cuimhneachadh obair a' chorrain
anns an fhoghar a bh'againn,
's tha 'n geamhradh gu bhith againn.

Ruins

There are ruins of houses down on the shore-plain, and the wan lazy-beds are sleeping in the oxter of the shore, and the great boats are rotting in the warping sun. On a summer's day, fifty years ago, the village stepped back a pace, and now the stolid grass-covered walls have taken root again, and the thatch has sagged, and the lazy-beds far from the shore are falling asleep, and it is almost summer.

The old woman who told me last year the story of the curing sheds, and the story of her own youth, and the story of the day before yesterday in the village, is sitting beside the hearth, and the evening is drawing in, and summer is almost upon us, and winter is almost upon us.

The old woman who told me last year a little of the story of the village is gleaning the days of spring, and threshing the oats in the barn, and grinding them with the quern she has kept, and remembering the sickle's work in the autumn we had, and winter is almost upon us.

An gàire mar chraiteachan salainn
ga fhroiseadh bho 'm beul,
an sàl 's am picil air an teanga,
's na miaran cruinne, goirid a dheanadh giullachd,
no a thogadh leanabh gu socair, cuimir,
seasgair, fallain,
gun mhearachd,
's na sùilean cho domhainn ri fèath.

B'e bun-os-cionn na h-eachdraidh a dh'fhàg iad
'nan tràillean aig ciùrairean cutach,
thall 's a-bhos air Galldachd 's an Sasainn.
Bu shaillte an duais a thàrr iad
ás na mìltean bharaillean ud,
gaoth na mara geur air an craiceann,
is eallach a' bhochdainn 'nan ciste,
is mara b'e an gàire
shaoileadh tu gu robh an teud briste.

Ach bha craiteachan uaille air an cridhe,
ga chumail fallain,
is bheireadh cutag an teanga
slisinn á fanaid nan Gall –
agus bha obair rompa fhathast
nuair gheibheadh iad dhachaigh,
ged nach biodh maoin ac':
air oidhche robach gheamhraidh,
ma bha siud an dàn dhaibh,
dheanadh iad daoine.

The Herring Girls

Their laughter like a sprinkling of salt
showered from their lips,
brine and pickle on their tongues,
and the stubby short fingers that could handle fish,
or lift a child gently, neatly,
safely, wholesomely,
unerringly,
and the eyes that were as deep as a calm.

The topsy-turvy of history had made them
slaves to short-arsed curers,
here and there in the Lowlands, in England.
Salt the reward they won
from those thousands of barrels,
the sea-wind sharp on their skins,
and the burden of poverty in their kists,
and were it not for their laughter
you might think the harp-string was broken.

But there was a sprinkling of pride on their hearts,
keeping them sound,
and their tongues' gutting-knife
would tear a strip from the Lowlanders' mockery –
and there was work awaiting them
when they got home,
though they had no wealth:
on a wild winter's night,
if that were their lot,
they would make men.

Aig Tursachan Chalanais

Cha robh toiseach no deireadh air a' chearcall,
cha robh ìochdar no uachdar aig ar smuain,
bha an cruinne-cè balbh a' feitheamh,
gun muir a' slìobadh ri tràigh,
gun feur a' gluasad ri gaoith,
cha robh là ann no oidhche –
is gu sìorraidh cha chaill mi cuimhne
air do chuailean bàn 's do bheul meachair,
no air an aon-dùrachd a shnaoidh sinn
ri chèile an cearcall na tìme,
far nach suath foill ann an tràigh dòchais.

Am Bodach-Ròcais

An oidhch' ud
thàinig am bodach-ròcais dhan taigh-chèilidh:
fear caol àrd dubh
is aodach dubh air.
Shuidh e air an t-sèis
is thuit na cairtean ás ar làmhan.
Bha fear a siud
ag innse sgeulachd air Conall Gulban
is reodh na faclan air a bhilean.
Bha boireannach 'na suidh' air stòl
ag òran, 's thug e 'n toradh ás a' cheòl.
Ach cha do dh'fhàg e falamh sinn:
thug e òran nuadh dhuinn,
is sgeulachdan na h-àird an Ear,
is sprùilleach de dh'fheallsanachd Geneva,
is sguab e 'n teine á meadhon an làir
's chuir e 'n tùrlach loisgeach nar broillichean.

At Callanish Stones

The circle had neither end nor beginning,
our thought had neither start nor finish,
the still universe was waiting,
sea not stroking the land,
grass not moving in wind,
there was no day, no night –
and I shall never forget
your fair hair and tender lips,
or the shared desire that wove us
together in time's circle
where treachery will not touch hope's shore.

Scarecrow

That night
the scarecrow came into the cèilidh-house:
a tall, thin black-haired man
wearing black clothes.
He sat on the bench
and the cards fell from our hands.
One man
was telling a folktale about Conall Gulban
and the words froze on his lips.
A woman was sitting on a stool,
singing songs, and he took the goodness out of the music.
But he did not leave us empty-handed:
he gave us a new song,
and tales from the Middle East,
and fragments of the philosophy of Geneva,
and he swept the fire from the centre of the floor
and set a searing bonfire in our breasts.

Leòdhas as t-Samhradh

An iarmailt cho soilleir tana
mar gum biodh am brat-sgàile air a reubadh
's an Cruthaidhear 'na shuidhe am fianais a shluaigh
aig a' bhuntàt 's a sgadan,
gun duine ris an dean E altachadh.
'S iongantach gu bheil iarmailt air an t-saoghal
tha cur cho beag a bhacadh air daoine
sealltainn a-steach dhan an t-Sìorraidheachd;
chan eil feum air feallsanachd
far an dean thu chùis le do phrosbaig.

Lewis in Summer

The atmosphere as clear, translucent
as though the veil had been rent
and the Creator were sitting, in His people's view,
at potatoes and herring,
with no one to whom He could say a grace.
Probably there's no atmosphere in the world
that offers so little resistance to people
to look in at Eternity;
there's no need for philosophy
where you can make do with binoculars.

LAURENCE GRAHAM

Flans Frae Da Haaf

Da wind flans in frae Fitful Head
Whaar dayset in a glöd
Hings ower da far haaf's wastern rim
Reeb'd red as yatlin blöd.

An flannin in fae dat black ert,
Borne in on flans o faer
Come cauld black tochts at numb da hert
An slokk da emmers dere.

O Loard abön, hadd Dy grit haand
Afore da daylycht dees,
Ower aa at ploo dir lonlie furr
Trowe dy wind–skordet seas.

O Loard, I pray, look kindly doon
An hadd Dy haand ower aa,
Till my lang–santet hert wins back
Whaar winds sall never blaa.

Whaar winds sall never blaa nae mair
Nor skies nae langer lour,
Whaar dayset laek some hamely haand
Smoors aa life's emmers ower.

Da wind flans in frae Fitful Head
Wast ower fae blatterin seas,
Bit never da lang, lang lippen'd sail
Whaar lycht an lippnin dees.

JACK RENWICK

High flyer

Sharlie o Skerpa's boy
Charles,
Brief-cased ta kill
Wi a sheaf o memoranda
At wid a shokkit his faider's coo
Boardin da plane at Sumburgh
Fir a wirkin lunch wi Sir Someen-ir-idder
Ta discuss oil.
Guid gaird me,
Hit's juist laek yesterday I mind his midder
Flyin ta Gord
Fur a scaar o sweet oil
Ta beek aald Sharlie's hainch
Whin he fell bakklins ipo da stove
Juist pleepin ida horrors o drink.
Yon most til a bön whaar
Charles
Got his laer aboot dis oil
Richt frae da girse röts, you micht say.

Winter comes in

Grey dawn brakkin ower troubled watters,
Da Soond laek a burn wi da rip o da tide;
Da Mull, black an grim ida first o da daylicht,
Wi da sea brakkin white on his nortmast side.

Yowes kruggin closs ida lee o a daek-end,
Creepin frae a chill at bites ta da bon;
Solan an scarf aa wirkin inshore,
A sign at da best o da wadder is don.

Hail sleetin doon wi a Nort wind ahint it,
Blottin oot laand an sea frae da scene,
An iron coortin closin ower aathing:
Winter has com ta da islands ageen.

STELLA SUTHERLAND

Aesy for Some

'Kek!' said da bonxie, gaen efter a maa,
an keppin da fish at da craetir let faa,
'dir nae need ta wirk whin dir fûles at'll do it,
an aa you mann do is ta schaest till dey spew it!'
'Oh, true, very true!' said da cuckoo,
'livin is aesy, if you only ken hoo!' –
an he heisted da idder eggs oot ower da side –
'dey'll hae ta geng, or I canna bide!'
An noddin his head, as if he agreed,
an hunklin his shooders wi tochts o da feed, –
'Every ane kens his ain wye best!'
said da craa as he robbit da laverick's nest.
Bit da laverick sprang ida lift, an sang:
'Never leet, life is sweet, an it winna be lang!'

At da Croft Museum

Robbie, whin I wis alang a while sinsyne,
du med me wylcome; I cam in trow, sat
i da hoodie shair i da shimley neuk.
Du played Da Sodger's Joy, Da Fairy Dance,
Da Mirry Boys o Greenland, Kail an Knockit Coarn,
fit aye nuggin, bow and fingers fleein.
Da paet-reek lay in flat fine-wadder drifts,
da röf wis tekkit neat an snug an tight,
an aa da gear wis dere ready for öse:
I could a taesed a laag an spun a treed,
or rubbit oot a brönnie or a bap;
du could a wund a simmind, run a lead –
dat wid a been 'in keepin' as dey hae't –
bit still hit wid a been a makadö.

For da tröth is, Robbie, dat day is by,
an aa dis gear sae lately wint wi öse
Time's flick is frozen lifeless, still as stane;
only da fiddle's no oot-dön, da tön,
da tön plays on; da draem, da draem moves on –

da draem o dem at no sae lang ago
clang tae dis rock, loved, toiled, failed, wöre awa –
an idder folk afore dem an benon –
dir lives an deaths makkin da laand we ken,
dir caandleflames lightin wirs for wir onn.

Dey kent dir simmer days o haet an honey,
hedder in bloom, boats i da eela calm,
fish at da flee, da line, da pock, da waa;
baess i da lang girse, sweet mylk in plenty;
da paet hill, clod an moss, taand for da mirk,
an möldy-bletts an cooses for da byres.
Aa da peerie toonship wis lood wi life,

Stella Sutherland

an da joy you canna buy wi ony money.
Sheep i da hill, oo for cairds, wheel an wires.
Da haaf, da sailin, love ta lippen hame
whin hairst drew on wi blashy-blinks an weet;
da mön at maets da corn ower da yard-daek,
heuk, scyde, made swaar, shaef, cole, stook, dess an scroo,
aa gaddered in an hirded i da yard;
tattie-cro, press an girnel lipperin ower,
(da millstanes gaen aroond dir timeless rant) –
da fiddle for da fjana an da foy,
da Sabbath psalm liftin da mind abön.

White winters cam, bitter upon ootliers –
skalva an flukker, hail an sleet an gale –
uplowsin, blots o watter, frost again.

Snug fae da blast, dey wrought athin da haand,
strae kishies, docken böddies, simminds wund,
cairdin an spinnin, makkin, spaekin ower
dir bits o plans – dir future – noo wir past;
an aa da time, da sang alang da blöd –
dey couldna hain, bit dey could haand it on.

Dey wir a vaam at cam ower aa da laand:
da aald fine wyes wis altered for da waar –
an O da winters o hert's bittersie,
Grund doon wi poverty an idders' greed!
Dir mortal frames could nedder win nor want,
sair riven wi fant, wi toarns o need an pride.
Schaested, debateless, driven benon dir strent,
some o dem geed, an some wis kerried oot;
some bedd, tho toom da hoose, da hert, da press,
da fiddle hingin sangless on da waa.

Aa gaddered noo in eart's green baand dey lie.
Fu mony kens or cares bit dee and me?

Dey böre an strave, gret sair, or keepit in –
better ae hert ta brak as aa da world ta winder!
Boady an braeth dey gae wis, an da foond
o aa at's wirs eenoo, an da regaird
we feel for aa at's right ta inward sense.
Dey yearned forever upward, laek da flooers
bund i da seed under black tons o time –
draemin o light, strivin towards da light,
an dybin on an on becaase dey most –

till dis caald eart sood tak a warmer cant,
an da frost melt an lat da simmer trow,
an burst dir laef, dir blossom an dir sang!

Da Time an Da Tön

Sharp an sweet, a tön
rins trow my head,
tho da fiddle's lang ootdön,
an da fiddler dead.

I hear da shudd an tread
o da shiftin shön,
see da lass at led
an da lad at followed on,

cledd i da dear new claes
at dey tocht sae braa,
noo muldert aa ta ess
an worn awa.

Steppin tae da time, da tön
aye bade dem on,
an it aye seemed far ower sön
whin da reel wis done.

Forgotten time's geen by
fae dey birled an set,
dat lass an lad at I
hae never met:

bit in my blöd an bane
dey meet — an mair —
löd, vynd an atfirts taen
fae mony a pair —

lightsome, or makkin maen
whin da mean days cam;
faithless — or fond an fain
till da last grey gam.

While da time an da tön rin true
generations pass,
and da sang i da blöd is ay new
ta some lad an lass.

ALASTAIR MACKIE

Three Tree Poems

(i)

Rodden Tree

In a neuk o the gairden
the rodden tree sproots,
a hingin armoury
o spear-heidit leaves.
Rodden berries o hard bleed
clot amon the spear heids.
Green and cramasy fend the hoose
and aathing inside and oot
fae the pirn-taed bogle, slater grey,
fae the beardit witch wi the claw-hemmer neb
fae aa the cronies o darkness.

The foonds o this hoose will never cowp.

(ii)

Uprootit Fir-Tree

A boat has foonert in the fir wid
amon the fern-bushes, the yowies' thooms
the Sargasso sea o drookit grass.
My feet and hands howk and cleuk,
my body showdin alang its beddit keel.
Aince a tall tap-mast
that took on the winds and gravity
for years and won.

Its reets, neebors to the worms,
are nou a skirl o shargert airms,

snappit tow o fibres
dumfoonert at the licht.

A nether world stares me in the face.
A jaggit circle,
a doup o mools and deid tap-reets.

(iii)

A Tree in Orkney, Stromness

Clock, sang-school, spinnly hand. Fae the winda,
near ten year I watcht ye be Atlas to the lyft
o Orkney – a brig o blue, a bilin
o blae cloods. And ablow ye hens noddit.

The seasons jowed their fower bells in your kirk.
You were the heichest roof in the haill toun.
A blackie on your tap-mast branch could sing
till a sky-line ruled by watter and flat parks.

Spring buds jabbit the air, the frost loupit.
In summer your leaves fattened. Syne the birds
pleept in your twisty groins. At the back-end
atween your strippit nieves the ness whitened.

Ye tellt the years; births, merriages, deaths, wrecks,
blindrifts, friendships, poems . . . Memories like
rings o your age are wappit roon ye. Viking mast
o the grey earth-fast langship o the toun.

IAIN MAC A' GHOBHAINN

FROM *Tha thu air aigeann m' inntinn*

Gun fhios dhomh tha thu air aigeann m' inntinn
mar fhear-tadhail grunnd na mara
le chlogaid 's a dhà shùil mhóir,
's chan aithne dhomh ceart t' fhiamh no do dhòigh
an déidh cóig bliadhna shiantan
time dòrtadh eadar mise 's tù:

beanntan bùirn gun ainm a' dòrtadh
eadar mise gad shiaodadh air bòrd
's t' fhiamh 's do dhòighean 'nam làmhan fann.
Chaidh thu air chall
am measg lusan dìomhair a' ghrunna
anns an leth-sholas uaine gun ghràdh,

's chan éirich thu chaoidh air bhàrr cuain
a-chaoidh 's mo làmhan a' slaodadh gun sgur,
's chan aithne dhomh do shiighe idir,
thus' ann an leth-sholas do shuain
a' tathaich aigeann na mara gun tàmh
'a mise slaodadh 's a' slaodadh air uachdar cuain.

IAIN CRICHTON SMITH

FROM *You are at the Bottom of my Mind*

Without my knowing it you are at the bottom of my mind, like one who visits the bottom of the sea with his helmet and his two great eyes: and I do not know properly your expression or your manner after five years of the showers of time pouring between you and me.

Nameless mountains of water pouring between me, hauling you on board, and your expression and manners in my weak hands. You went astray among the mysterious foliage of the sea-bottom in the green half-light without love.

And you will never rise to the surface of the sea, even though my hands should be ceaselessly hauling, and I do not know your way at all, you in the half-light of your sleep, haunting the bottom of the sea without ceasing, and I hauling and hauling on the surface of the ocean.

(Translated from the Gaelic by the author)

Owl and Mouse

The owl wafts home with a mouse in its beak.
The moon is stunningly bright in the high sky.

Such a gold stone, such a brilliant hard light.
Such large round eyes of the owl among the trees.

All seems immortal but for the dangling mouse,
an old hurt string among the harmony

of the masterful and jewelled orchestra
which shows no waste soundlessly playing on.

The Clearances

The thistles climb the thatch. Forever
this sharp scale in our poems,
as also the waste music of the sea.

The stars shine over Sutherland
in a cold ceilidh of their own,
as, in the morning, the silver cane

cropped among corn. We will remember this.
Though hate is evil we cannot
but hope your courtier's heels in hell

are burning: that to hear
the thatch sizzling in tanged smoke
your hot ears slowly learn.

The White Air of March

This is the land God gave to Andy Stewart –
      we have our inheritance.
There shall be no ardour, there shall be indifference.
There shall not be excellence, there shall be the average.
We shall be the intrepid hunters of golf balls.

Have you not known, have you not heard, has it not been reported
that Mrs Macdonald has given an hour-long lecture on Islay
and at the conclusion was presented with a bouquet of flowers
by Marjory, aged five?
                Have you not noted
the photograph of the whist drive, skeleton hands,
rings on skeleton fingers?
                Have you not seen
the glossy weddings in the glossy pages,
champagne and a 'shared joke'.
                Do you not see
the Music Hall's still alive here in the North? and on the stage
the yellow gorse is growing.
                'Tragedy,' said Walpole, 'for those who feel.
For those who think, it's comic.'
                Pity then those who feel
and, as for the Scottish Soldier, off to the wars!
The Cuillins stand and will forever stand.
Their streams scream in the moonlight.

Poem of Lewis

Here they have no time for the fine graces
of poetry, unless it freely grows
in deep compulsion, like water in the well,
woven into the texture of the soil
in a strong pattern. They have no rhymes
to tailor the material of thought
and snap the thread quickly on the tooth.
One would have thought that this black north
was used to lightning, crossing the sky like fish
swift in their element. One would have thought
the barren rock would give a value to
the bursting flower. The two extremes,
mourning and gaiety, meet like north and south
in the one breast, milked by knuckled time,
till dryness spreads across each ageing bone.
They have no place for the fine graces
of poetry. The great forgiving spirit of the word
fanning its rainbow wing, like a shot bird
falls from the windy sky. The sea heaves
in visionless anger over the cramped graves
and the early daffodil, purer than a soul,
is gathered into the terrible mouth of the gale.

Old Woman

And she, being old, fed from a mashed plate
as an old mare might droop across a fence
to the dull pastures of its ignorance.
Her husband held her upright while he prayed

to God who is all-forgiving to send down
some angel somewhere who might land perhaps
in his foreign wings among the gradual crops.
She munched, half dead, blindly searching the spoon.

Outside, the grass was raging. There I sat
imprisoned in my pity and my shame
that men and women having suffered time
should sit in such a place, in such a state

and wished to be away, yes, to be far away
with athletes, heroes, Greek or Roman men
who pushed their bitter spears into a vein
and would not spend an hour with such decay.

'Pray God,' he said, 'we ask you, God,' he said.
The bowed back was quiet. I saw the teeth
tighten their grip around a delicate death.
And nothing moved within the knotted head

but only a few poor veins as one might see
vague wishless seaweed floating on a tide
of all the salty waters where had died
too many waves to mark two more or three.

Nothing Will Happen

Nothing will happen surely in this village
except adultery, sickness, harmless lies.

Listen, I watch the suns in their redness,
winding imperially around our stone,

and the absent-minded minister taking a walk
through these green clouds of his philosophy.

Nothing will happen surely . . . What's that?
Our crayon books are torn by strange shell fire.
A voice is shouting. There is nowhere safe.

And a dog digs for its bones under the holly.

The deer look down with their clear questioning eyes.

IAN HAMILTON FINLAY

Orkney Interior

Doing what the moon says, he shifts his chair
Closer to the stove and stokes it up
With the very best fuel, a mixture of dried fish
And tobacco he keeps in a bucket with crabs

Too small to eat. One raises its pincer
As if to seize hold of the crescent moon
On the calendar which is almost like a zodiac
With inexplicable and pallid blanks. Meanwhile

A lobster is crawling towards the clever
Bait that is set inside the clock
On the shelf by the wireless – an inherited dried fish
Soaked in whisky and carefully trimmed

With potato flowers from the Golden Wonders
The old man grows inside his ears.
Click! goes the clock-lid, and the unfortunate lobster
Finds itself a prisoner inside the clock,

An adapted cuckoo-clock. It shows no hours, only
Tides and moons and is fitted out
With two little saucers, one of salt and one of water
For the lobster to live on while, each quarter-tide,

It must stick its head through the tiny trapdoor
Meant for the cuckoo. It will be trained to read
The broken barometer and wave its whiskers
To Scottish Dance Music, till it grows too old.

Then the old man will have to catch himself another lobster.
Meanwhile he is happy and takes the clock
Down to the sea. He stands and oils it
In a little rock pool that reflects the moon.

The English Colonel Explains an Orkney Boat

The boat swims full of air.
You see, it has a point at both
Ends, sir, somewhat
As lemons. I'm explaining

The hollowness is amazing. That's
The way a boat
Floats.

Mansie Considers the Sea in the Manner of Hugh MacDiarmid

The sea, I think, is lazy,
It just obeys the moon
— All the same I remember what Engels said:
'Freedom is the consciousness of necessity'.

Voyage

As brave as any admiral
Yet snug as little Moses
I sailed on darker-than-the-tide
The ship of my neurosis.

I almost wanted to be wrecked;
My eyes were full of wonder
As in the stern I stood erect,
A merman on a flounder.

My course was most aesthetic, sailed
To show against the sun.
'Fishface' I'd call to battleships
But did not meet with one.

Blossom Quarry, Rousay

'Blossom' they call this quarry of grey stone,
Of stone on stone on stone, where never white
Blossom was sweetly blown; wet dynamite
Would blossom more than seeds in this place grown.

And yet as Blossom Quarry it is known.
And who knows but the namer named it right?
Its flowers are on the hand with which I write:
Bent backs, sore bloody blisters it has grown.

RHODA BULTER

Shetlandic

Sometimes I tink whin da Loard med da aert,
An He got it aa pitten tagidder,
Fan He still hed a nev-foo a clippins left ower,
Trimmed aff o dis place or da tidder,
An He hedna da hert to baal dem awa,
For dey lookit dat boannie an rare,
Sae He fashioned da Isles fae da ends of da aert,
An med aa-body fin at hame dere.

Dey 'lichted fae aa wye, some jöst for a start,
While some bed ta dell riggs an saa coarn,
An wi sicca gret gadderie a fok fae aa ower,
An entirely new language wis boarn.
A language o wirds aften hard tae translate,
At we manna belittle or bö,
For every country is prood o da wye at hit spaeks,
An sae we sid be prood a wirs tö.

Bül My Sheep

We geng ta da kirk an gie wir alms,
We say wir prayers an we sing wir psalms,
An whin a hoose is blindit an murns a daeth
We veesit da folk an we send a wraeth,
An slip da bairns a penny or twa,
Dan blyde whin wir oot an awa fae it aa.

We coulda dün somethin ta shaa we wir carin
Whin we heard o da lass at wis hae'n a bairn,
An we mighta steadied da craiter a bit
At drank himsel silly juist tryin ta forgit,
An sae for da waant o a haand ta clesp
He wis left ta redd oot his ain reffled hesp.

We sit at da hertstane an creeticise
Dis eens claes an da nixt eens wyes,
An maskin truth wi a bit a fun
Say 'God be blissed at wir no laek yun',
An rowe in ower da bed content
At anidder day wis nobly spent.

An whin we read o da rivers at ran wi bluid
An da fok at wir sufferin fae aertquake an flüd,
Did we send twartree shilleens ta aese dir state,
Ta help ta git medeecine, shaalter an maet?
Or shak wir heads an say 'Dear a dear,
Loard be praised at it's no laek yun here'?

It's aesy whin snug i wir ain fower waas
Ta wave wir flag an support da caase,
Bit aa ower aften we staand at da brink,
Faert ta spaek oot for whaat neebors wid tink,
An seekin nae pairt in anidder's affairs,
We staand idda shadoos an offer wir prayers.

'O Loard be wi aa dem in trouble dis night,
An send someen ta guide dem an shaa dem a light.
Provide for da poor wi fantation oppressed,
Ta da seek an da waakrife gie paece an rest.
Send help ta da needy whaarever dey be,
Bit I canna win, sae You needna send me.'

Bit my, whaat a different place dis wid be,
If we aa set wis doon an towt whaat we could gie.
If we didna hae money, gie wir time for a while;
Say twartree kind wirds, mak a man smile;
Or juist ta be dere an patiently listen
Ta somebody's troubles, is truly a blissen.

Dan geng ta da kirk an gie wir alms,
Say wir prayers an sing wir psalms,
An whin we come oot again hae a care
For aa da fok at we didna see dere,
For ta serve wir Maker is ta help een-anidder,
An aye traet da man at we meet laek wir bridder.

DÒMHNALL MACAMHLAIGH

Fèin-Fhìreantachd

Chan iarr iad orm ach
gal aithreachais peacaidh
nach buin dhomh
's gum faigh mi saorsa
fhuadan nach tuig mi:

ludaradh ann an uisge
an dèidh uisge tana, guinteach
am feallsanachd;

agus gun amharas chrochadh iad
an nigheadaireachd anns na nèamhan.

Soisgeul 1955

Bha mi a-raoir anns a' choinneamh;
bha an taigh làn chun an dorais,
cha robh àite-suidhe ann
ach geimhil chumhang air an staidhre.

Dh'èist mi ris an t-sailm: am fonn
a' falbh leinn air seòl mara
cho dìomhair ri Maol Dùin;
dh'èist mi ris an ùrnaigh
seirm shaorsainneil, shruthachrsa:
iuchair-dàin mo dhaoine.

An uair sin thàinig an searmon
– teintean ifrinn a th' anns an fhasan –
bagairt neimheil, fhuadan
a lìon an taigh le uamhann is coimeasg.

Is thàinig an cadal-deilgeanach na mo chasan . . .

DONALD MACAULAY

Self-righteousness

They ask of me only
to weep repentance for a sin
that does not concern me
and I shall get in return an alien
freedom I don't understand:

to be drubbed in one thin,
wounding water after another
of their philosophy;

and confidently they would hang
their washing in the heavens.

Gospel 1955

I was at the meeting last night;
the house was full, packed to the door,
there was no place for me to sit
but a cramped nook on the stairs.

I listened to the psalm, the tune
transporting us on a tide
as mysterious as Maol Duin's;
I listened to the prayer,
a liberating, cascading melody:
my people's access to poetry.

Then we got the sermon
– the fires of hell are in fashion –
vicious, alien threats
that filled the house with confusion and terror.

And I got pins-and-needles in my feet . . .

A' Cheiste

'Carson,' their iad,
'a chaitheas tu d' àm a' dèanamh dhàn? –
b' fheàrr dhut, air a' cheann thall,
a bhith ri ceàird eile.'

An ceann thall
dhòmhsa
a rèir an slat-thomhais-san.

Ghineadh dhomh faillean,
à spàirn dhìomhair;
dh'fhàs e tromham craobhach;
chuir mi romham gum fàsadh e dìreach

gus buil thoirt air slatan fiara.

Question

'Why,' they say,
'do you spend your time making poems? –
it would benefit you more, in the end,
to practise another trade.'

The end
for me
measured by their yardsticks.

A tree was for me engendered
by some mysterious striving;
its branches spread through me;
I decided it should grow undeformed

to overcome deviant yardsticks.

ALISON PRINCE

Rough Sea

Old deaths are one with air and spray,
The taste of salt and the scattered sun
Glinting like fish scales
On the body of the sea.

The dead are everywhere.
They are the curled life in the gull's egg,
The rain, the leap of dolphin
Or the whale whose vast tarpaulin back
Gleams briefly through the wave.

The dead live on while anyone
Shifts to balance the sea's heave,
Watches its surge loom up,
Lean and swing under
While the next wave looms again.
The dead have known this wet skin
And the muscles' ache, the sense
Of where the still horizon lies
Beyond these sea-hills.

I am the dead.
There is no fear of fear
In this wild sea.

Hens

We could not keep hens
after the mink scheme failed.
The quick, slim murderers in unsold fur,
released from their cages, set about
feasting on cygnets, gull chicks
and the treasured eggs
of herons, wrens and our homely hens.

A more mysterious scheme
brought dead seals to the beaches.
The mink too met a death unseen,
their dark, soft fur shrouding
the delicate constructions of their bones
deep under black rocks, sometimes found
by digging, puzzled dogs.

Now comes the newly severe scheme
to clip small wings while sharp-beaked, brutal birds
cruise the skies of commerce, greedy-eyed.
Parents mourn their dead hopes for loved hatchlings –
but our island hens
shuffle and croon, and kindnesses
warm the hand like strong-shelled new-laid eggs.

Having no Cattish

The cat fits in the crook of my arm
as would a new-born child, although
equipped with wariness.
He cares for me much as I care
for what seems to be God, demonstrably
here and in charge
though often deaf to prayer.
Having no Cattish, I cannot explain
why I wear clothes, speak words and cause
a car to move, but as a cat will choose
food and a kind hand, not the frosted wood,
I trust in the unknowable
rather than cry on the cliff's edge
to a diagram of stars.

MAVIS GULLIVER

From one island to another

Sometimes
there is nothing
to show there's land
across the sea.

When clouds convert to mist
that sits
on the sea's surface,
the mind relies on memory
to add the lines of islands,
the rise of distant hills.

When mist drifts and lifts,
the outlined islands,
shapes of distant hills
emerge like wraiths,
like shadows of themselves,
until sun scalpels through,
reveals each detail
sharp
against a blue so clear,
the miles of ocean
seem to disappear
and I could walk
across the water.

AONGHAS MACNEACAIL

oideachadh ceart

do john agard is jack mapanje

nuair a bha mi òg
cha b'eachdraidh ach cuimhne

nuair a thàinig am bàillidh, air each
air na mnathan a' tilleadh a-nuas
às na buailtean len eallaichean frainich
's a gheàrr e na ròpan on guailnean
a' sgaoileadh nan eallach gu làr,
a' dìteadh nam mnà, gun tug iad gun chead
an luibhe dhan iarradh e sgrios,
ach gum biodh na mnathan
ga ghearradh 's ga ghiùlain gu dachaigh,
connlach staìle, gu tàmh nam bó
(is gun deachdadh e màl às)

cha b'eachdraidh ach cuimhne
long nan daoine
seòladh a-mach
tro cheathach sgeòil
mu éiginn morair
mu chruaidh-chàs morair
mun cùram dhan tuathan,
mu shaidhbhreas a' feitheamh
ceann thall na slighe,
long nan daoine
seòladh a-mach,
sgioba de chnuimheagan acrach
paisgte na clàir,
cha b'eachdraidh ach fathann

AONGHAS MACNEACAIL

a proper schooling

for john agard and jack mapanje

when i was young
it wasn't history but memory

when the factor, on horseback, came
on the women's descent from
the moorland grazings laden with bracken
he cut the ropes from their shoulders
spreading their loads to the ground,
alleging they took without permit
a weed he'd eliminate
were it not that women cut it and carried it home
for bedding to ease their cows' hard rest;
and there was rent in that weed

it wasn't history but memory
the emigrant ships
sailing out
through a fog of stories
of landlords' anguish
of landlords' distress
their concern for their tenants,
the riches waiting
beyond the voyage,
the emigrant ships
sailing out
a crew of starved maggots
wrapped in their timbers,
it wasn't history but rumour

cha b'eachdraidh ach cuimhne
là na dìle, chaidh loids a' chaiptein
a sguabadh dhan tràigh
nuair a phòs sruthan rà is chonain
gun tochar a ghabhail
ach dàthaidh an sgalag
a dh'fhan 'dileas dha mhaighstir'
agus cuirp nan linn às a' chladh

cha b'eachdraidh ach cuimhne
an latha bhaist ciorstaidh am bàillidh
le mùn à poit a thug i bhon chùlaist
dhan choinneamh am bràighe nan crait
gun bhraon a dhòrtadh

cha b'eachdraidh ach cuimhne
an latha sheas gaisgich a' bhaile
bruach abhainn a' ghlinne
an aghaidh feachd ghruamach an t-siorraidh
a thàinig air mhàrsail, 's a thill gun òrdag a bhogadh,
le sanasan fuadach nan dùirn

cha b'eachdraidh ach gràmar
rob donn
uilleam ros
donnchadh bàn
mac a' mhaighstir

cha b'eachdraidh ach cuimhne
màiri mhór, màiri mhór
a dìtidhean ceòlar
cha b'eachdraidh ach cuimhne
na h-òrain a sheinn i
dha muinntir an cruaidh-chàs
dha muinntir an dùbhlan

it wasn't history but memory
the day of the flood, the captain's lodge
was swept to the shore
when the streams of rha and conon married
taking no dowry
but david the servant
who stayed 'true to his master'
and the corpses of centuries from the cemetery

it wasn't history but memory
the day kirsty baptised the factor
with piss from a pot she took from the backroom
to the meeting up in the brae of the croft
not spilling a single drop

it wasn't history but memory
the day the township's warriors stood
on the banks of the glen river
confronting the sheriff's surly troops
who marched that far, then returned without dipping a toe,
clutching their wads of eviction orders

it wasn't history but grammar
rob donn
william ross
duncan ban
alexander macdonald

it wasn't history but memory
great mary macpherson
her melodic indictments,
it wasn't history but memory
the anthems she sang
for her people distressed
for her people defiant

agus, nuair a bha mi òg,
ged a bha a' chuimhne fhathast
fo thughadh snigheach,
bha sglèat nan dearbhadh
fo fhasgadh sglèat
agus a–muigh
bha gaoth a' glaodhaich
eachdraidh nam chuimhne
eachdraidh nam chuimhne

and when i was young
though memory remained
under a leaking thatch,
the schoolroom slate
had slates for shelter
and outside
a wind was crying
history in my memories
history in my memories

gàidheal san eòrp

1
oisean mac fhinn
('ic a' phearsain)
am pòcaid gach saighdeir

2
buanaphairt an grèim
air eilean naomh eilidh
mac fhinn 'ic a' phearsain
cur meanbh-bhlàths
an lomnochd a thìm

3
bheartar btrònach
a' suathadh
ri chridhe
nan lide bog leighseach
oisean mac fhinn mar chungaidh

4
eadar eachdraidh is uirsgeul
an gàidheal ag imeachd
thar raointean thar shléibhtean
an gàidheal ag imeachd
eadar cliù is caitheamh
an gàidheal ag imeachd
an gàidheal ag imeachd

tiodhlac feirge

na h-uaislean is na h-eilthirich
nach iad a rinn an sgrios oirnn

na h-uaislean is na h-eilthirich
nach iad a rinn am feum dhuinn

a gael in europe

1

ossian son of finn
(and macpherson's)
in soldiers' pockets

2

imprisoned buonaparte
on saint helen's island
son of finn and macpherson
putting a hint of warmth
in his naked time

3

sorrowful werther
massaging
his heart
with soft healing syllables ossian
son of finn as balm

4

between fact and fable
the gael travelling
across plains and mountains
the gael travelling between fame
and exhaustion
the gael travelling
the gael travelling

the gift of anger

the gentry and the foreigners
was it not they who crushed us

the gentry and the foreigners
was it not they who saved us

am fìor mhanaifeasto

an eaconomaidh

tha sinn cho sultach, *ars thusa ri*
baile nan cnàimhneach

gnìomhachas

deasaichidh sinn
airson an t-saoghail ùir thu

seo do chaibe
seo do dhèile

dìon

tha feum air ar laoich
son èiginn ('s dòcha) is ga-rìribh
ann ur n–uairean slaodach

cèineachd

brisidh sinn claigeann
troiche uabhasaich, eagal 's gu
sèid e oirnn le anail fuamhaire

foghlam

sgrìob d' ainm air sglèat
àireamhaich tàirngnean
leugh do chunntas

the real manifesto

the economy

we're so well off, *says you to*
the city of skeletons

trade and industry

we'll prepare
you for the new world

here's your spade
here's your plank

defence

we need our heroes
for emergencies (perhaps) and certainly
when there's time on your hands

foreign affairs

we'll crack the skull of
some terrible dwarf, lest he
blast us with giant's breath

education

scratch your name on a slate
enumerate nails
read your invoice

home

blind man
came to the isle, said
now i have parameters
i hear the surf
i hear the birds   my eyes
can't map which way
they come   my hands
can't tell their shape
the voices of   the wind
and birdsong tell me
all i need to know

EDWARD CUMMINS

Buckie Man

The boatman said he'd join the Brethren.
Somewhere he'd seen a light above the mast.
They pointed at his house. I wondered when
He'd come to know his last drink was his last.

The ropes plopped into the water, calmer now
Than we had known for days. We hauled them in
As sounds that make the sea washed clean our bow.
We coiled the ropes. My thoughts remained on him

His forebears mended nets at that same gate.
It swings both ways, to failure or reward.
Experience is just and those who wait
See wonders in the deep they call *The LORD*.

He told me once the Lewismen had laughed:
'Poor Buckie Man, his home's before the mast'

Moray Firth, 22–2–93

MAOILIOS M. CAIMBEUL

Eileanan

Eileanan ag èirigh às a' chuan,
am bunaitean falaichte
ann am fiosraichidhean cèin.

Tha eileanan ann an tìm, 's iad às,
nan treòraichean don ànrach,
no meòrachadh air tìm nach till air ais.

Tha feadhainn ann a tha suidhichte,
àrd is dubh ann am meadhan na tuil.
Cha ghluais an doineann an staid chruthaichte.

Is feadhainn le àmhghar làbha is pronnaisg,
leanabain mhara nan cridheachan sract'.
Is eileanan deighe fuar ghluasad anns an uisg'.

Seasaidh cuid gun ghuth a radha,
aonranach — am broinn a-staigh na creig —
gun iad a' gèilleadh do theas an latha.

Tha thusa nad eilean anns a' chamhanaich,
deimhinne, dorcha, diùltach,
do bhunaitean ann an tìm a theich.

Agus mise aig dol sìos na grèine,
eilean a' coimhead air eilean eile.
Fàgaibh mi agaibhse ur dealbhadh fhèin.

MYLES CAMPBELL

Islands

Islands rise from the sea,
their foundations hidden
in ancient experiences.

Islands are in and out of time,
guides for the wanderer,
or submerged in time long gone.

Some well-established,
high and dark in the flood.
No storm will affect their formation.

Some in lava and sulphurous grief,
sea children of torn heart.
And others, icebergs, coldly moving in the water.

Some will stand silent,
lonely – inwardly as rock –
unassuming in the heat of the day.

And there is an island in the dusk,
assured, dark, repelling,
its foundations in a fading time.

And this island in the sunset,
island watching another island.
You decide your own form.

An t-Eilean na Bhaile

Ann an dòigh 's e baile a th' ann am Muile,
ann am baile tha na treubhan measgte.
'S e baile th' ann le sluagh sgapte
mar a tha an saoghal a' fàs gu bhith na bhaile,
na seann luachan, treubh is cinneadh,
a' seargadh ann an saoghal gnìomhachais, teicnigeach.

Chunnaic mi dà chloich nan seasamh nan aonar –
chaidh lianag fhàgail dhaibh anns a' choille ghiuthais,
clachan 's dòcha a thogadh nuair a bha a' ghealach naomh,
iad nan seasamh mar dhà phrionnsa, no prionnsa 's a ghràdh,
nan clachan-cuimhne do shìol rìoghail.
Treubh a chaidh à bith.

Chunnaic mi clach eile – Dòmhnall Moireasdan, Àird Tunna,
ceithir fichead 's a còig deug, is 'inntinn geur mar sgithinn,
làn de sheanchas is bàrdachd a threubha,
colbh sgairteil de Chlann na h-Oidhche,
agus timcheall air am baile a' fàs –
baile nach tuig e – luachan do-ruigsinn dha chèile.

Tha am prionnsa na chloich anns a' choille,
agus treubh ùr air a thighinn.
Chan eil rìgh nam measg a dhearbhas
a threòir.
Is tuath iad le cridheachan pàipeir;
pàtaranan faoine a' losgadh.

Cha dèan na mnathan gaoir tuilleadh, is an t-eilean na bhaile.

The Island a Town

In a sense Mull is a town,
in a town the tribes are mingled.
It is a town of dispersed people
as the world grows to be a town,
the old values, tribe and kin,
withering in an industrial, technological world.

I saw two stones standing alone –
a lawn was left for them in the pine wood,
stones perhaps raised when the moon was holy,
standing like two princes, or a prince and his love,
memorial stones to a seed royal.
An extinct tribe.

I saw another stone – Donald Morrison, Ardtun,
ninety-five years of age, mind sharp as a knife,
full of the history and poetry of his tribe,
stalwart column of the Children of the Night,
and round him the town growing –
a town that does not understand him – values that
                                        cannot be bridged.

The prince is a stone in the wood,
and a new tribe has arrived.
There isn't a king among them to prove
his valour.
They are a peasantry of paper hearts;
empty patterns burning.

The women will lament no more. The island is a town.

Dà Ghuth

Tha dà ghuth annadsa agus annamsa,
Crìosda agus Cù Chulainn,
aon umhail, aon ceannairceach,
fear uasal an irioslachd,
fear uasal an calmachd,
fear a ghabh Nietzsche ris,
fear a stamp e fo chasan:
e faicinn gràdh, urram, ùmhlachd
mar nithean a thruaill spiorad
agus inntinn sluagh na h-Eòrpa,
gam fàgail bog, eisimeileach.
Ach cha do rinn a ghaisge feum dha.
Bhàsaich e air a chrann-ceusaidh fhèin,
an inntinn shoilleir ud
glan às a ciall.

Bàrd Baile?

Bàrd baile, dè 'm baile?
Bhruidhinn mi an-diugh ri fear à Kyoto,
thig, 's dòcha, e-phost à Wagga Wagga.
Tha lìon a' chòmhraidh
eadar Illinois is Mandalay,
eadar Port Rìgh is Parramatta,
Cha robh mo sheanmhair,
tha mi cinnteach,
a-riamh a-mach à Stafainn.
A-nis, chan eil Paris ach shìos an rathad.

Twa Voices

Twa voices ye hae, and I hae:
voices o Christ an Cù Chulainn.
Yin bousome, yin heidie,
yin mensefu wi lowness,
yin mensefu wi derfness,
yin that Nietzche tuik tae himsel,
yin that he strampit ablow his fit –
him that saw love, honour, bousomeness
as clarts tae fyle the spreit
an ingyne o Europe's fowk
an lea them dowf an merghles.
But whit the better wes he o his bauldness:
he died on a cross on his ain,
thon ingyne skyrie-bricht
clean gyte.

                          (Scots version by Derrick McClure)

Village Poet?

Village poet, what village?
Today I spoke with a man from Kyoto,
perhaps an email will come from Wagga Wagga.
There's a web of conversation
between Illinois and Mandalay,
between Portree and Parramatta.
My grandmother, I'm sure,
was never out of Staffin.
Now, Paris is just down the road.

Yesnaby

No trees at Yesnaby,
no whole rock either:
siege-guns of the centuries
have blasted their weather.

Here is a place
sheer for self-murder,
sliced away like losing face,
feet splashed away under.

Here is a place
for desperate lovers,
like lumps of cold swell
breaking over each other.

Here is a place
for fulmar and artist,
impassively pinioning
the blue loose canvas.

Here is a place
for the capsized ewe,
feet feeble against blackbacks
that cornwall her eyes.

Here is a place
for the repulsed poet,
grinding his alliteratives
with a shaped pestle.

No trees at Yesnaby,
no whole rock either:
siege-guns of the centuries
have blasted their weather.

Orkney Movement

The sun sets
a fat candle
to flicker on the damask sea.

The ebb slips
an oyster
down the Atlantic throat.

The spume off Braga
is unbottled
bubbly.

Dale's silage towers
are green
as flowers:

their cows
make fudge
and whisky.

And no sooth news
can break
the silent

editorial
of swell and gull,
as Vikings close the door

and settle to a feast
they roar low after
like Buccaneers.

John Aberdein   119

NORMAN BISSELL

Slate, Sea and Sky

An island on the rim of the world
in that space between slate, sea and sky
where air and ocean currents
are plays of wild energy
and the light changes everything.

Sounds

Sometimes here
it's hard to tell
the sound of the wind
from the sound of the waves
or the sound of the waves
from the sound of the rain
or the sound of the wind
and the waves and the rain
from the sound of my breath.

To Take a Boat Out

To take a boat out
one summer's day
would be fine
and to hear again
the creak of oars
in their rowlocks
their feathered dip
in the sea
would be even finer
and out in the firth
to ship the oars
and lie back
and listen
to the chortle of water
under varnished oak
would be finer still
and to let the boat
drift with the current
wherever it might go
that warm blue day
no words can say.

CHRISTINE DE LUCA

St Ninian's Isle

Hit hed ta be a saint at strayed dis far nort
at cared aboot da sowls o Pictish fisherfock.
Foo da bairns o Rörick man a gawped
at men at biggit chapels, walked in silence.
Someen man a shaan dem whaar da piltocks took
Sweyn Holm, Selkie Gyo; gied dem bere an kale
fae Ireland's strippit rigs or Bigton's toons.
Eence here, dey nivver could a left: trist slaked
wi beauty; air laced wi saat an honey.

St Francis could a felt at hame here if he'd come
ta Ninian's Isle. On a warm day he micht
a tocht himsel on some green suddern shore.
Da burnin pavements o Assisi couldna kyemp
wi dis pale nordern straand: a glisk on watter
is hit kissed da sheenin saand; a smush
o saandiloos aroond his feet, chastin froad
alang da shörmal is he gud. He wid a traded
martins fur a single laverock i da lift
sheerlin blissins on göd an ill alick.
An i da waa o Ninian's kirk he wid a fun a font
filt wi a stirlin's laachter. An i dis quiet place
a wagtail micht a tippit in ta sit wi him
– is shö sits apö da altar noo – her flicht
a peerie chancel dance wi dips an tirls
at's lifted centuries o haerts. She'd be
his perfect cantor for a chorus o göd wirds.

Here, on a boannie day, wi birds apö da wing
aa but da herdest haerts could fin demsels
communin wi da greater scheme o things.

Viking Landfall

A pride o langboats
wast fae Bergen
wi draems o land
an lipperin kyists o mel;
spirits lift is Shetland rises
low apö da prow, an Viking een skile
shores fur meids, telt o
bi winter fires.

Ta starb'rd
da bicht o Uyeasoond
whar Thor rived Fetlar
wi his tirn nev, an balled her
clean soothbye;

dan roond bi Hascosay
ta peerie Aywick
an deeper Otterswick;
an on ta Gossabrough:
a gentle daal, wi hoop o sand
an tang ta sweeten soorest aert;
a burn fur water an a mill
an space ta bigg an dell.

Der sails wir lowered, oars aesed,
boats couped owre fur kye ta platsh ashore
an aa da proil o conquest
o mankind owre aert
wis lowsed apö da saand.

Dey'd mak der mark at Gossabrough.
In Norrawa, der saga wid be rösed
roond idder fires.

Paet Wark

Voar wark dön, tochts turned ta da hill,
tae a hairst o winter paets ta cut an cure:
faider'd set oot wi tushkar an wi spade
ta rip an flae an cast a bank or twa.
Dellin doon, liftin fae da soolp,
tushkar fleein, paets wheefed up an owre;
ootburg spreadin, dark daek risin:
rings o movement an even lines o aert:
a dance, a vynd wrocht oot
in space an time
sin fire first lowed.

Licht lentenin days, sun high apö wir backs,
we'd burst apö da hill
liftin da larks;
raise da mossy paets laid oot apö da broo,
dan set apö da daek, blue brittle brack.
Banks raised, we'd loup clean owre
– peerie legs aye langer, jumpin farder –
spang owre skyumpies
platsh da greesy greff.

As simmer opened oot, da aert cam dry
an greffs wir raised. We'd roog
an turn da half-dry paets, but aye fin time atween
ta tirl an headicraa, curse motts an mudjicks,
seek berries, shaste mooratoogs,
purl i da paety loch
an swittle taes.

Ta tak paets hame, a hidmost wrastle at da hill:
we'd rummel roogs, bag, borrow, fill kishies high
rinnin wi dem, kyempin, ta da rod;

hark an hear da tractor a dizzen times afore he cam
– aye late, a day's wark dön, a dizzen mödoos maa'd –
an whit a styooch o hentin, firin,
ballin bags on tap, maakin da lod.

As mirknen creepit in
we'd clim on tap
an ride da cuggly lod
lik monarchs.

Hame wi da hirdin, black paets
sookit herd an dry: a glöd
o winter warmth fae simmer's haand:
a varg, a strug, a spree:
a smile o simmer aert an sun an wind rowed up
ta hap da caald.

JIM MONCRIEFF

Slow to Return

Love's season
Is a warm need to sing
Hardwood floors
And dancing with high heels
Mini-skirts
And back-combed hair

Love's season
Is a memory of old movies
Railway stations
Slow trains to Devon
And walking on water
With mayflies

Love's season
Is a tired skin
Pinched between the fingers

Slow to return

Time to Dream

When you're gone
The Dutch chair
And my print of the Sun Flowers
Will sit together

Chrome yellow sunshine
Will pour through my window
Against the cobalt blue horizon
As I face towards Foula

And memory
Will paint the walls
Of the sun-room that you never saw
With tree-lined avenues
Windmills
And children skating
On frozen canals

The brick-maker's art
Will warm my corner
And the smell of roast coffee
Pervade the room
As I sit in the rocking chair
From Mangaster
And watch you cycle past
On the way to your mother's house

Cutting Corn

Your hands made the blade sing
Working the stone
My fingers ran the sharp edge
Honed to perfection

Your hands made the blade sing
In the morning sun
Its arced length quivered
Then danced among the corn

Gently behind me
You cut my shadow down
As we moved out together
On a warm edge of time

Your hands made the blade sing
Wetting the stone.
My fingers run the sharp edge
Cutting deep my memory

Jim Moncrieff   127

CATRÌONA NICGUMARAID

Sireadh

Choisich mi mach
   air cladaichean ciar mo bheatha
's dh'amhairc mi air creagan mo shòlais . . .

Is an uair sin,
      dìreach mar sin,
            chunnaic mi puill mo dhòrainn
— tuinn mo nàdair, sìos is suas,
   gu na rionnagan no chun na h-uaigh,

a' plapail dìreach tiotan bhuam
no sgrìobadh fad' air falbh mu Eilean Heàrlais,
   null, thall bhuam, aig Eilean Heàrlais.

Is an uair sin, gille-brìghde
   a' coiseachd gu speirgeach air an tràigh
   gun suim aig'
      — ochan, ochan,
         brìgh mo bhàrdachd,
         brìgh mo bhròin, m' uallach 's m' ochan.

Ruigeadh m' anam mach gu Eilean Chanaigh
   thar nan ulbhagan gun smaointinn,
   a' flodadh suas mun an Taigh-Sholais,
   sìos seachad Meall a' Ghrìobaidh,
   null an uair sin chun an Stob Iullan,

a' lorg m' anam is mi a' sireadh,
mi fhìn air chall le tachdadh amhaich
   — deòir neònach 'na mo bhroilleach
   nach tuit gu bràth
   gu Là na Cruinne,

CATRIONA MONTGOMERY

Seeking

I walked out
   on the dusky shores of my life
and I viewed the rocks of my joy . . .

And then,
   just like that,
      I noticed the pools of my anguish
– the fluctuating waves of my character, rising and falling,
   to the stars or to the grave,

palpitating a little distance from me
or stretching far away by Harlosh Island,
   far, far away, by Harlosh Island.

And then, an oyster-catcher
   arrogantly patrolling the beach
   without concern
     – my God,
      for the essence of my poetry,
      my anguish and my sighing.

My soul would wander to the Isle of Canna
   over the waves without concern,
   floating up by the Lighthouse,
   down past Meall a' Ghrìobaidh,
   over then to the Stob Iullan,

searching for the soul, and seeking
the self who is lost with a choked heart
   – strange tears
    which will never be shed
    till the Day of Judgement,

strì, 's a' strì ri siubhal an Duine,
mi fhìn, mi fhìn 's mi dol á follais
    sìos, sìos chun à' ghrunna,
's a' togail ceann an-dràst 's a-rithist . . .

    O Thì – mise! mise!
    Sgìth! sgìth! mise! mise!

    Dè 'n t–ioghn',
      dè 'n t–ioghn',
        ars an t-isean.

striving and striving to follow the Self,
myself, myself as I disappear
    down, down to the dark depths,
my head bobbing up now and then . . .

    My God, my God, I am exhausted,
    I am exhausted.

    No wonder,
      no wonder,
        sang the bird.

LAUREEN JOHNSON

Staandin sten

Staand ida lee o a staandin sten,
look at da stars
an tell yoursel it's da 21st century.
Tak your radio,
tune as you will.
Tak your mobile,
an 'phone a friend'
fae da lee o a staandin sten.
Mak a daet, phone hame,
tell your midder you'll be laet
fae da lee o a staandin sten.
An when da batteries gie oot,
da server goes doon,
an every last sowl you ken
is geen ta bed,
lift your eyes
ida lee o da staandin sten
an see foo da stars is turned
da sky aroond
while your night fled.

Shore skippers

I never in my life at I can mind o
axed onybody what der faider's job wis.
But ida sooth, when I wis at da college,
dey aye axed me – an sometimes, axed nae mair.

It seemed, for some, a most important question
an laekly it wis what der folk wis laerned dem.
I fan it queer, an no whit I wis wint wi,
for aa at wirfolk ever axed wis names.

Weel, what's his surname? Kens du wha his folk is?
As, twenty year ahead, it's me at's axin.
An tho I say I fin it interestin
(an sae it is) I ken it's something mair.

An tho I'm always seen it far superior
ta axin for da colour o da collar,
ta judge ee generation be anidder,
we aa sood mind, haes certain shortfaas tö.

An noo I see we're at da sam game raelly –
shore skippers, tellin ower da meids at we kent
an tryin ta trace da coorse wir bairns is sailin
afore dey sail awa clean oot o sight.

An I wid laek da bairns o da class-conscious
ta laach an pey as little heed as my eens,
wha skyimp, an say *Oh Mam, dat's no important!*
an geng back ta der world o Christian names.

MORAG MACINNES

A Masterpiece of Amazing Realism

For the first time ever, sculpting that truly rivals Mother Nature!
Cheemo the Crofter, perfect and precious
in every detail, in collector vinyl quality, hair rooted
meticulously by hand for a totally
natural look.

Cheemo has his own knitted 'toorie bunnet' and distressed
denim 'breeks'. Remove his 'woolly pulley' to reveal
homespun 'combinations'. His 'takkity beuts' are a miracle of
miniaturisation, walk him
on stone for the authentic sound of toil. He comes complete
with 'tuskar', 'creel' and string of 'cuithes'.

Demand will be great: send no money now.
Simply return the Reservation Application to
Historic Scotland.
This doll is not
a toy. He is a fine collectable.

Mrs Orkney interviewed

Lobban rocks, them
twirmie faced giants
fired me intae the roost.

Them wi their black big boy
bad moods, red knuckles, holed kishies,
they skairted me aal ower,
dropped me doon in a ruckle
no even tidy – wise! Me Ooter Isles wis

every which wey! A bairn would've done better an wi
less noise. Hid's teen a while tae
redd mesel up right – I'm punished be
watter, hid slaps
till I greet.

See the henge that's me waist? Laced tight in the middle,
just lukk at the lift
o me hips! This ribs is stone bone, sharp as
shards,
an owld owld heart in their kist.

I'm no denying
the tattoos – I wis young then, and
brandit aal ower wi twigs. I'm prood o the dragon
but there some names I'd rather forgit.
I'm gettan worn doon noo – lossan teeth
(Ah'm got false eens! The buks calls them Replicas, sez
they're as good.
Weel, no if thu's
me.)

Aal's no bad tho.
Wait fur June. Thu'll catch me
dilderan, kitleens on me
midden, the gowans an dogflooers
runnan amuk on me knows.
Ah'm rowed in the
highflying yarn o me lavros.
Them's me
dozy days, I lukk
aboot seventeen.

The Superhero in Scotslit: a submission for my Masters

You sup it up, don't you, the brose o it. How he
hit the high road, mother in a – mutch is it? –
moothan at the ben end, under the requisite
rowan, 'don't forget yer spurtle!'
Drink them hardy hurdies doon, the meal bag burstin
on his peat hill shoulder. Snoosh him in,
he's rampin Reekwards as you read. Donald.
Ranald. Allan, Callum, in a skirt. With a
dirk.

Licky, licky, awful sticky, that
coo candy. Walter's lad o pairts, puir but
richt passionate, under the paintit
mountains. Howk in the steam o him
ploshin a stream in the fairnteckle glen, the fish birlin
uphill in wilderness under his skirt. That bunnet's
chuist awesome wi antlers – no, read it again, yon's
a deer up ahint him. If the flash o boy knees
in the bracken makks you slaver,
beware! That's tame fare. Steady noo –

Gardieloo!
Here's hussies in howffs, deils an anatomists waitin to
pounce on the douce. Murdo an Hector, doggin aroond
in a clapshot o psalmsong an sex in a boxbed. What wi
debtors, the dice an delirium, mammie's meal's at the
back o the press. There's curds in the whey. This
peedie spurtle's grown a thistly heid: it's cock
a leekie time. Petticoat tails, rich pickins in middens, fill up
a poke o them!

Spiced up, b'ilt through, strings lowsed, how'll
wur clootie dumpling slice? Micht he
mak money fae dirt, build a pad fur a nabob, die fenced up
wi angels in Hawick Pretoria? Fire a bridge ower a wilderness,

send all his shares tae a bank in Drumsheugh? Or, kiltie
cauld bum, see red on the Baltic an leave no a crumb
for his wake? Grease on his endpapers; nary a fight
ower his final slice?
Whit? You're fur sicconds? Had on –
there's aye a bap in wur oven.

MÒRAG NICGUMARAID

Geamhradh

Ribeagan gaoiseideach
ro lag airson am
boinne driùchd a ghiùlan.
Biastagan liatha
's iad lag, reòidhte.
Cluaran is clachan.
Bogalach is fraoch.
Bileagan a bhàsaich
mus d'fhuair iad aois.

MORAG MONTGOMERY

Winter

Hairy strands
too weak to bear the
dewdrop.
Grey insects
that are weak, frozen.
Thistle and stones.
Bog and heather.
Shoots that died
before reaching maturity.

(English version by Ronald Black)

SHEENAGH PUGH

Days of November 2009

Short days, long shadows:
sun rising low skims the hill.

Mending, making good, days full
of outdoor jobs, folk

racing to finish before dark,
before winter. Angled light, always

on the edge of leaving. These days
when every little thing feels urgent,

unmissable, when all you want
is to hold on to a lit rack

of cirrus, the taste of woodsmoke
catching your throat, a sleek seal

slipping back under, the farewell
of geese, scribbled in black arrows.

Come and Go

He has chosen, far nearer the end
than the beginning, to live
where, every day, he can watch the land

come and go, each time gleaming as if
it were new made. Sandbars shoulder
into the sun, their whereabouts too brief

to map, never drying out. Under
its pulsing skin the sea echoes
sunlight, shadows the clouds, goes undercover

in mist. What it is to be bodiless,
boneless, to reshape, to fill
with yourself the moulds of coves and bays,

take yourself back. He walks mile
after mile, blanking aches, stays up late
in the blue half-light, resists the pull

of sleep while he can, while his sight
still serves him, before that jerry-build,
his body, can no longer house a spirit
still nowhere near done with the world.

Dresden Shepherdesses of 1908

They pose in their carnival costume,
gazing patiently into the lens,
waiting to be fixed for all time

as a group of china figurines.
The four in front, seated, arrange crossways
their dainty crooks, twisted with ribbons,

whose lattice pattern mirrors the laces
on their bodice fronts, below the frills
of the spilling collars, below the faces

crowned with roses, framed in tumbling curls,
the heavy features that don't pretend,
for a moment, to be other than male.

It's plain too in the way they stand,
the six at the back, grounding their crooks
like rifles. Tight-laced, white-gowned,

they plant their boots foursquare and black
beneath flounced skirts. Mothers and wives
have been busy with a pattern book,

letting out waists, lengthening hems and sleeves
to make them look perfect; you can see
the pride they take. Stepping out of their lives

for one night, the night they can be
who they like, alter themselves to fit
whatever otherness takes their fancy,

clerks and boatmen assume the exquisite
frivolity of ornaments, the dress
of a past time, choosing to inhabit,
for this one night, their inner shepherdess.

GORDON DARGIE

At Bannaminn: voar

I know to reach the top of course we climbed
but looking back is what I first remember.
I cannot find the time before my mind
would fix events in their familiar order
and when we did not know what lay before us,
as if the wind had blown away the words
I never found again, caught on some fence
or down the banks, was it like that, when first
we went to Bannaminn and up the hill
and did not know then Minn would be special.
Unsentimental weather started tears
that make the scene so bright. As usual
there is no one is on the beach although
I watch the children's tracks and where they'll go.

At Bannaminn: hairst

They did not play that day, they were not born.
I watch where they would play, have played, still play,
and never more could see this beach without them,
as tethered as the bairns once were on Havra
to stop them falling off, but all departed.
And now I cannot see the man and woman
they became without seeing how they started.
And empty as the houses are at Minn.
No one is an island but anyone
can be a valley, water pouring in.
A slow long wave of mist floods down the hills,
lit pink from underneath, into Clift Sound
and over this skiddling of islands
soon rime cold in a grey Atlantic swell.

ANDREW GREIG

Shetland

He sailed for Shetland, near the edge,
to bog & cliff & a celibate friend.
She did her helpless best by him.
He climbed all day and failed to fall.

Light-hoarding stars above her bed,
a full moon on the wall – he wanted to be dead,
and badly. *A mortal sin*, she said, *I tried it*.
Well, she was Catholic but that stuck.

No way out but up. At the crux
he clutched into the chimney's heart and heaved . . .

He taped his knuckles, she poured wine.
Just reflected light this tenderness, but still
that night they lay like pardoned thieves – baffled, eased,
beside her paper moon, beneath her fading stars.

Orkney / This Life

It is big sky and its changes,
the sea all round and the waters within.
It is the way sea and sky
work off each other constantly,
like people meeting in Alfred Street,
each face coming away with a hint
of the other's face pressed in it.
It is the way a week-long gale
ends and folk emerge to hear
a single bird cry way high up.

It is the way you lean to me
and the way I lean to you, as if
we are each other's prevailing;
how we connect along our shores,
the way we are tidal islands
joined for hours then inaccessible,
I'll go for that, and smile when I
pick sand off myself in the shower.
The way I am an inland loch to you
when a clatter of white whoops and rises . . .

It is the way Scotland looks to the South,
the way we enter friends' houses
to leave what we came with, or flick
the kettle's switch and wait.
This is where I want to live,
close to where the heart gives out,
ruined, perfected, an empty arch against the sky
where birds fly through instead of prayers
while in Hoy Sound the ferry's engines thrum
this life this life this life.

Andrew Greig   145

Stromness Evening
(for George Mackay Brown)

Sun's sloped off across slack water,
haar wreathes the Sound of Hoy.
We could call each day a wager
but the books are closing now.

My neighbour's in his doorway
playing blues harmonica –
not that he's unhappy,
it's just what he does well;

you can tell by the manner
the notes stretch and prowl
like stray dogs long after
he's stopped – the way

a man's still thought on
as Calum knocks out his harp
and we glance, silent a moment,
at a certain dark window on our way to the pub.

Papay

And we see at last how beautiful it was, how small,
as though memory keeks down from where we never were –
the shell-sand beach, the seaweed tastefully arranged

about the lovers sprawled by rising tide,
your belly's beat absorbing mine
as though the whole shoreline were breathing.

One might think happiness a tidal island,
reached at times whose tables
don't appear in the national press.

We must leave the sickle bay
while we still can. On the sand
we stare where seals have lain –

they left a hollow, shining as it fills.

JIM MAINLAND

Avoiding the Mitford Sisters

When I have nothing to say, my lips are sealed.
David Byrne
The following tone is a reference tone . . .
Don Van Vliet

So I followed myself to the end of the line
where to get a signal you had to string up
a riggy-bane, a circuit squadron of wire
out of Braque out of Etch-a-Sketch
out of Zigzag Wanderer
over the ceiling and under the picture of the family
from the house of blue lights;

or get on the roof to line up the correct
sonar genuflection and earth it
into the ghost of the red telephone box.
The missed calls from the nineteen fifties,
all weather and homespun hypocrisy.

Some nights the static spoke in tongues:
Hilversum, Keynsham, Elysium;
some nights a scrap of Jimmy Giuffre,
a moonstruck instrumental madrigal;
and sometimes a warmer sound sleeved
in eelskin, issuing the Sargasso swish.

Then a week and a day eating
what gets blown in, raw:
icterine, subalpine, pomarine,
blue phase fulmar – rumoured
to be hallucinogenic –
and treasured from the beach
a barbershop tourniquet,
a raddled isotopic delicacy.

Now let in only a little arthritic morse,
a ring-loop hiccup of lo-fi skiffle-smoke;
then binge on silence, and sieve its complaint
through a small bellows
so that it almost breathes, like this:

bom bom dip da dip da dip
bom bom dip da dip

But enough preliminaries.
Time to stop answering the door,
stop lifting the phone from its contaminant.
A cormorant flies in with semaphore;
a fieldfare finds me the flags for fuck off.

A Child Lifts the Shell of the World to her Ear

The excavations have unravelled nothing. According to our
tallymen, these were a different species: savage, oracular.

Nothing like us. What armoured their hearts, our instruments
will disclose. Likewise their unguarded poor, their fetish for the sea.

But such a thin reliquary! Only a shiver of static resounds
with the staves and hoops of rigs and reels that was their sound.

These seams of religion, stripes of ceremony, stains of commerce
from the sediment: a dull bullion not worth the salvage.

The years we wasted trying to isolate the properties
of the extra 'a' in 'waand', the redundant 'p' in 'uploppm'.

Lulled by the first rippled silence, thrown by a spoor of gutturals,
we followed the lure of this sun's acre, hoping to find ourselves;

now only one exhibit remains, which we can make nothing of,
so long out of its element: the forlorn pollen of love.

Jim Mainland   149

Prestidigitator

Watch this, watch my hands, look in my eyes:
this is viral, this is fiending, this is Celebrity Smash Your Face In,
I'm spooling tissue from an ear, I'm sawing her in half, no, really,
I'm vanishing your dosh, I'm giving it makeover, giving it bonus,
palming it, see, nothing in my hand, open the box, check out
your divorce hell text tease sex tape, whoops,
gimme a tenner gimme your valuables this is a hammer this is
                                                      an explosive
see the cleverdazzle off the mirrorgleam, moat me that you peasant!
over here, here, oy you, break-up Britain, toff off! watch this instead,
it's my way, it's bodies out of the hat, watch out, that's had
                                                      your legs off
this is brainsmear this is scorcher this is dying doing the job
                                        you loved this is
pure dead victim

The Devil's Music

The girl from the croft sings *All Shook Up*
As she churns. This butter, if it comes,
Will be bewitched, she mourns. Dreams.
Her lips are like a volcano top.

Her weary plout picks up the backbeat.
Take the profit from the lot,
Let the whole island syncopate!
A burning hand feeds the snout

Of her breast. A man barks. A dog laughs.
Even the glimpsed sea jinks at the words,
As its preposterous Atlantic quiffs

Drop in a swither of curds,
Like the wedding dress dream
Of Mhairi, his latest flame.

The Gunnister Man

I knew him, Horatio

I came across a photo of you aged three or four,
squinting into the sun: you and your mother
and I think that must be your sister.

Nothing in that gaze gave notice of the days
ahead, of course. And nothing could ease
their so much weight and weeping anyway.

Except your music, and that came much too late.
I'm hearing you say, *Look at me now, mate,*
a whoreson whose songs sell real estate.

*

In the gardens of Bapaume the dead elbow out
still, their bones clacking like crockery. *I hate
this life. If I could just win home,* you wrote.

If I had the gift, I'd spring you through a portal
into bracken, crowned in rowan or myrtle,
pierced a hundred-fold, immaculately immortal,

and on the run, from yourself: a rumoured spectre
roaming the moor, taking quit rent to the Factor.
A version of you is sung by metal detector

and ringtoned to a man, climbing a hill,
bright and early, ghosting between the will-
o-the-wisp and the whip-poor-will,

between the hairst blink and the horse-gock,
and a sudden psychedelic
uproar of the whaup and the lark.

*

There was the usual gossip about a tryst,
about something toxic in the enfolding mist,
and a scar that never healed across each wrist;

perhaps he'd turned a head or two in town,
his skin was too expressive of the bone,
the diligent carrier of a defective gene.

*

In the abandoned lodge where we repair,
clods crumble and topple in a blue peat fire,
and row after row of hosiery exhaling there.

ALISTAIR PEEBLES

Burn

for Yasuko and Eiji, in Orkney

I'm trying to explain 'burn' to Yasuko,
and its difference from 'brook'
and their difference in turn
from 'river' and 'stream'.
And she nods . . .

I make widths with my hands
from six feet to inches,
announcing each word,
getting carried away into
'rivulet', 'brooklet', 'beck', 'rill' and 'ditch'
– this last between finger and thumb.
She repeats them, carefully,
but we're still not quite there.

'England is . . .?'
'Brook.'
'What is "burn"?'

Then I show them a photograph,
taken today on a walk in the hill.
'Ah, burn,' she says, smiling,
and I think that we've got it.
But, 'What's that?' asks Eiji.
'That's a track,' I say.
'That's a burn, and that's a track.'
Both blue in the February sun.
And we laugh, for the track's
flooded with snow-melt
and yesterday's rain . . .

It's a burn.

AONGHAS PÀDRAIG CAIMBEUL

Geàrraidh na Mònadh à Smeircleit

Taigh Fhionnlaigh,
Taigh a' Bhadhlaich,
Taigh Aonghais a' Cheanadaich,
Taigh Aonghais 'ac Dhòmhnaill,
Taigh Alasdair Ruaidh,
Taigh an Ruaidh,
Taigh Dhòmhnaill Eachainn,
Taigh Sheumais Shlàdair,
Taigh a' Chlachair,
Taigh Sheonaidh Mhòir,
Taigh Alasdair Dhuibh,
Taigh Phàdraig Eòghainn,
Taigh Sheonaidh Ailein,
Taigh Dhòmhnaill Penny,
Taigh Iagain Dhòmhnaill.

Mar a bha,
's mar a tha,
's mar a bhitheas.

Fad saoghal nan saoghal.

Amen.

ANGUS PETER CAMPBELL

Garrynamonie from Smerclate

Finlay's house,
The Benbecula man's house,
Angus son of the Kennedy's house,
Angus MacDonald's house,
Red Alasdair's house,
Domhachann's house,
A Ruaidh's house,
Donald Hector's house,
Seumas Shladair's house,
George's house,
The Stonemason's house,
Big Johnny's house,
Black Alasdair's house,
Patrick Ewen's house,
Seonaidh Allan's house,
Donald son of Penny's house,
Iagan Dhomhnaill's house.

As it was,
is,
and will be.

World without end.

Amen.

Ag Iasgach a' Mhic-Meanmna

Air madainn Samhna,
a' tighinn tarsainn Bràigh na Teanga,
chunna mi tràlair a-muigh sa Chuan Sgìth.

Ring-netters m' eanchainn,
sgadan drithleannach mo chuimhne,
agus an cuan cho mòr, 's cho àlainn, 's cho farsaing.

Stad mi mionaid
aig Bealach an t-Sliachd
a' cur lìon thairis air mo smuaintean.

An sluagh air an glùinean,
an Eaglais,
agus an cuan domhainn gar cuartachadh.

Fishing the Imagination

On a November morning,
coming over Upper Teangue,
I saw a trawler out in the Minch.

The ring-netters of my mind,
the glittering herring of my memory,
and the ocean so big, and so beautiful, and so wide.

I stopped for a moment
at the Brae of Humility
flinging a net over my thoughts.

The people on their knees,
the Church,
and the deep sea surrounding us.

Eòin

Rounded,
you begin life's voyage.

Somewhere,
where God breathed life into the very dust,

you were linked with a moment, a woman, a page, a poem.

I Love You

is the bird that has just taken off,

your high heels spicing behind me,

the black mantilla and the shawl,

the auburn hair and the drawn lines
spelling out 51 Glendales this new summer-time.

The Magic Clock

Do not ask for coffee
my darling
but take me
to that play area of your heart
where the smooth slide glides
and the wooden trains chug on time
beneath the penguin clock
where we have constantly embraced
waiting for the hour to strike
and the magic doors to open
to reveal
a monkey on a tree
a lamb on a roundabout
and a dolphin flying high

for in the coffee shop
my darling
I stabbed a needle through my arm
and sank into the flames again
on a final day without beginning
that may never end
this hellish separation
that has left a fearful chasm
and a religious bridge
between the innocent and the guilty
the toy shop and the coffee shop
where you play and I sip coffee
until the next hour strikes
and the magic doors open again
to reveal
a monkey on a tree
a lamb on a roundabout
and a dolphin flying high.

Do not ask for coffee
my darling
but take me
to that play area of your heart
where the smooth slide glides
and the wooden trains chug on time
beneath the penguin clock
where we have constantly embraced
waiting for the hour to strike
and the magic doors to open
to reveal
a monkey on a tree
a lamb on a roundabout
and a dolphin flying high.

SIÙSAIDH NICNÈILL

Iona, West Beach on a Rainy Day

An old left shoe, lost overboard.
An expensive trainer it was once, too.
The knot still tied.
Where's the foot, I wonder?

A frog flattened by the road.
Arms and legs as they last flapped.
An Atlantean survivor
finally tattooed by rubber tread.

Rocks of red and bright pale green
finely etched by sand and weed.
The golden grains and dark, dark wrack
thrown up like a stallion's mane.

A final hard scramble up to *Dun I*
to reach a well on the roof of the soul.
Heather scratched and fenced in
at every turn –
                    I retreat.

MÀIRI NICGUMARAID

Baile Ailein

Leam thu
Baile beag mo chiad cheum sgoile
Mo chiad chearcall charaidean
'S mo chiad dhealbh
Mo chiad phàirtidh
'S mo chiad dhannsa
Mo chiad turas oidhche bhom dhachaigh
'S mo chiad chianalas ag iarraidh as

Leam thu
Baile fada clachach cam
Le do thurachan-tharachan sluaigh
'S do chòmhlain threubhan annasach
De dhaoine a bhuineas
Is daoine nach buin
Is daoine nach gabhadh gnothaich
Ri cuid seach cuid

Leam thu
Le do sheann bhòidhchead
'S do sheann lùidearachd
Do ghàrraidhean cloiche
'S do thobhtaichean truagh
'S eadar làraich a sia deug
'S còig deug thar fhichead
Choinnicheadh mo sheanmhair 's mo sheanair
A phòsadh

Leam thu
Le do chnocan beaga creagach
'S do shaoghal fheansaichean is gheataichean
Is bhodaich bheaga chritheanach
Nach robh mar sin chun an-dè
Is tiùrran chloinne ag èigheachd 's a' ruith

MARY MONTGOMERY

Balallan

You are mine
Little village of my first step at school
My first circle of friends
My first picture
My first party
And my first dance
My first night-trip away from home
And my first longing to leave

Mine
Long stony ramshackle village
With your topsy-turvy population
And your bizarre tribal groupings
Of people who belong
And people who don't
And people who'll have nothing to do with either

Mine
With your old beauty
And your old bedraggledness
Your stone dykes
And your sad ruins
And between plot sixteen
And thirty-five
My grandfather and my grandmother met
To wed

Mine
With your small rocky hills
And your world of fences and gates
And of small shaky bodachs
Who until yesterday weren't like this
And hordes of children shouting and running about

Mu chuairt
Far nach robh iadsan a bharrachd
Chun an-dè
Is dè a-rèist an diofar?

'S ged a shaoil mi chun an-dè
Gun taghainn nad aghaidh
Seo sinn fhathast
A' conaltradh.

An Taigh-Tasgaidh 's an Leabhar

Feumaidh mi dol chun taigh-tasgaidh
dh'fhaicinn uidheam m'eachdraidh
a shad mo sheanmhair às
a shuath mo sheanair
le bhoisean cnapach sgìth
air a' chuairt mu dheireadh
a ghabh e
dhan t-sabhal.

Feumaidh mi dol chun taigh-tasgaidh
às aonais duslach an fheòir
air m' aodach,
dh'fhaicinn uidheam m'eachdraidh
mus tèid an leth-shealladh
den leth-sgeul
a th'agam
a dhìth
leis an sguab a th'air cul mo shàil.

Feumaidh mi leabhar bhithdeas air mo shùil,
de bhriathran nan làithean a dh'fhalbh,
feumaidh mi leughadh fo chomhair an àm
tha cànan an cunnart dol balbh.

Feumaidh mi leabhar a dh'innseas dhomh sgeul
nach eil idir air bilean an t-sluaigh,
a dhol gu fear eile 'son barrachd de dh'fhios
's de thuigse air adhbhar na truaigh'.

Where they weren't either
Until yesterday –
And so what does it matter?

And although until yesterday I thought
I would choose against you
Here we are still
Communicating.

The Museum and the Book

I must go to the museum
to see the tools of my history
my grandmother threw out
my grandfather stroked
with his tired knobbly hands
on the last round
he made
of the barn.

I must go to the museum
without the dust of the grass
on my clothes
to see the tools of my history
before the half-sight
of the half-story
I have
is swept
away by the brush at my heels.

I must have a book for my eyes
of the words of days gone by,
I must read it when facing the time
a language threatens to go dumb.

I must have a book that will tell me a story
that's not on the lips of the people,
must go to someone else for more information
and understanding of the reason for grief.

IAN STEPHEN

I'll Boil The Kettle

I'll boil the kettle since the mainlight's on,
breaking areas of angle-poise arcs
on colour-coded panels of contacts.

The skipper of the 'Golden Sheaf' can
pass the tow by radio-telephone:
'Over to you, Calum, at Loch Sealg.
The bacon and eggs are on below
and I'd better see about getting a crust
to share between the boys on Friday.'

That tone is set against the residue
of another task, a further latitude,
clear of the Butt and at eight degrees west.
A crewman simply went over the rails.
He jumped out to the calm night.
They threw fluorescence, lowered a boat.

We sent a chopper with potent spans
of live lights. It found only
lit buoys and flotation as
a brash litany of failed hopes.

Bothy – Taransay Island
(for Ewan Macrae, Creelfisher and Ferryman)

It had a sort of dead quality –
when he beached here before, in Uidhe Bay.
A place quiet because the people left.

Maybe it was the refurbished gables
that offended him or the sharp roof
before he even saw the Meccano system

of T and A pieces to take bolts
in live joists and rafters. Or maybe
he didn't like the scent of creosote

stealing downwind from the shelter.
It could have been the direct nylon red
of socks drying on Taransay stone.

If I was trying to go back,
pushed by six horses of the Suzuki,
I'd rather go further than the ruins

and cramped hints of cultivation.
There were five souls in 1961,
descended from rumoured hundreds.

After his spiel I need to know
from archives more adequately housed,
what they sowed and what evicted them.

DONALD S. MURRAY

The Girl Who Taught the Fisherman to Read

The girl who taught the fisherman to read
cut him loose upon a drag and swell of words
as powerful as any that laid siege
to his vessel when a dark storm swayed the world,
swirling till a rockpool was disturbed
by a corpse who shared his skills and trade, the screech and
     wings of gulls.

The girl who taught the fisherman to read
made him long to know these letters painted white
on boats tethered at the quayside – 'LK', 'SY', 'PD' –
and find out what careless pleasures consonants might hide
behind each careful brush-stroke. The rocking motion of the
     tide
seemed to promise rhythms he hoped might stir his nights.

The girl who taught the fisherman to read
anticipated gratitude and kisses for her time
giving meaning to his harbour – each
chart now understood, each fish-box and warning sign –
only to find out he had slipped her net, their lives not now
     entwined,
and a girl from 'LK', 'SY' or 'PD' has snared him on her line.

Language

Gaelic was sewn into us like grains
of oats, turnip-seed, split potatoes
ploughs folded below earth each spring.

It took root among the small talk
villagers stacked at peat-banks
or found gleaming in green fields,

Or when the sharp blade of their tongues
cut through each crop of scandals
that was the season's harvest in some homes.

Yet now croftland lies fallow.
Winds keen through rush and nettle.
Cold showers of thistledown blow

Where potatoes stalked and blossomed
and the words of English broadcast on the air
find strange, new seed-beds on our lips.

Ness Social Club, Fivepenny Machair

(near the Butt of Lewis)

Beer foamed like the near Atlantic
when we sat in that bar
which you – my city friend –
declared was the nearest
that you'd ever come
to this world's farthest end.

And these words made me think,
for between throatfuls of drink
I swallowed there
were times I heard
Shonnie speak of Sydney,
Murdo muttering of Mexico
and Donnie talking about years ago
when he'd spent days in Durban,
Hamburg, Tokyo.

The whole world spun
till I could see
huge and red at nightfall
sun
slipping down the window,
out of reach
as it spilled a thousand colours
on machair, wave and beach.

And it wasn't just drink talking
when I swirled down my beer
and said, '*The farthest end?*
The world could find its centre here.'

YVONNE GRAY

Cragsman

High on the stac you stand starfished
above the swell and thrash of waves
that churn and dissolve
the rocks below. Fulmars lift
from cliff ledges eyeing you
as they hang on the wind
in their aerial ballet.
Spine arced you poise
in a grotesque arabesque
balance honed by decades
at the rock face clinging
between sea and sky.
The pose you have struck
grows large in the dying light.

Nousts

A ferry weaves
among islands. Her wash unfurls –
laps at empty nousts

At night a trawler looms
at the pier – rust bleeds
from her floodlit hull

Waves slap harbour walls.
Dive boats and creel boats jostle
on the rising tide

The new marina gleams –
steel-armed pontoons wait
to berth summer yachts

Sunlit ships slip by
on the skyline – bright Babels,
crates stacked high on deck

At the head of the geo
fading nousts wait for boats
to come home

ROBERT ALAN JAMIESON

Glunta (A fisherman's prayer)

Dir is nae end: tides turn, i da var,
Bullin aboot wis: logos.
Saat lines da livin,
We cast up quhite wyrms.

Glunta pu's on: lichts weigh, aa wir gaer,
Aald quhite face: logos.
Saat lines da howlin,
We unert blue stonn.

Glunta, owre aa,
Be under Ert,
Mak fast wir motion,
Turn daeth.

Glunta, cover aa,
Be owre Ert,
Mak fast wir motion,
Weigh life.

Shore Poem

At the shore, my boy's hand
Wrote poetry, not recorded in a book,
But pure accounts of mood
Formed in clay on a flat stone
When the tide was out.

Joy on a day when I was happy.
I moulded its form and accepted its passing.
Grief on a day when I knew nothing.
I made it clay-real in the air and found release.

To be washed from a flat stone
When the tide came in.
The time to which that word applied
Washed with it, while the stone
Was smooth as the bone of my skull.

T' Scallwa Castle

Quhitever shite drappt oot dy privvies
Still maer bed on ahint, inside de,
In da trots an haas an guts
O da Stewart clan at aaned de.

I canna celebrate dy stonn in ony tongue
Nor care tae rub da green fae yon bress plaet
Da National Trust sae carefilly hae nailed ta de.
Fir evry chisel swap, a bairn gret oot fir maet.
Fir every stonn lade t'dy foond, anidder stonnless
Grave wis fillt wi benklt brukkit bens o fok
Still young if de an aa dy hertless kyn hed
Only hed a tocht bit eence fir somethin idder
Dan dir gut-fat laanded swallys an dir privvy shite.

Frisk Waatir Troot

Afoar he lærns t'sykil a byk
he's tentilie rowin da flatboddim
roond an aroond Melbie logh.

Siks jieir aald
an dark pætie waatir's
slappin at da syd.

He's wurriet 'at sumien myght kiek
fæ da quhyt-waasht hoos
akross da girssie mødoo an sie

waatir siepin in aboot
his rubbir bøt fiet –
an he'd gjit a lugfoo

quhan he wan hem,
fir no tellin oniebodie
he lækit denchir tø.

MEG BATEMAN

Iomallachd

Chan eil iomallachd sa Ghàidhealtachd ann –
le càr cumhachdach
ruigear an t-àite taobh a-staigh latha;
's e luimead na h-oirthir
a shàraich na daoine
is a chuir thar lear iad
a tha gar tàladh an-diugh,
na làraichean suarach a dh'fhàg iad
cho miannaichte ri gin san rìoghachd.

Och, an iomallachd, càit a bheil thu?
Càit ach air oir lom nam bailtean,
sna towerblocks eadar motorways
far am fuadaichear na daoine
gu iomall a' chumhachd,
an aon fhiaradh goirt nan sùilean
's a chithear an aodann sepia nan eilthireach
(a bha mise riamh an dùil
gum biodh an Nàdar air dèanamh àlainn).

MEG BATEMAN

Remoteness

The Highlands are not remote any more –
with a powerful car
you can reach the place in a day;
it is the bleakness of the coast
that wore the people down
and sent them overseas
that draws us today,
the miserable sites they left
as desired as any in the land.

Alas, remoteness, where are you?
Where but at the bleak edge of the cities,
in the towerblocks between motorways
where people are removed,
edged out from power,
the same hurt squint in their eyes
as is seen in the emigrants' sepia faces
(that I had fully expected
Nature to have made beautiful).

Tiodhlacadh Shomhairle MhicGill-Eain

27.11.1996

Bha d' eilean gun tu beò ann fo shneachda
fhathast mar a shnaidh thu e,
is daoine a' tighinn thugad san eaglais
is cha neo-fhreagarrach am beannachadh,
oir ged a lean thu ri rian eile
cha neo-ionann an duilgheadas
a bha aig Crìosd san uaigneas sa Ghàrradh
is agad fhèin air àird a' Chuilithinn.

Ged nach buin mi dha do threubh-sa
tha mi toirt taing dha do mhàthair,
dhan Taghadh nach tug leis thu
latha foghair san fhàsach,
airson bòidhchead aodainn is eilein,
airson ceòl na pìoba is na cànain
san d'fhuair thu lorg air a' ghaisge
's air maitheadh dhur cuid àmhghair.

Ged a tha thu glaiste gu h-ìseal
is clach-chinn dhut Sgùrr Alasdair,
is fad' o chrìochan do dhùthcha
togar do dhùirn ris an aintighearnas;
ged a lathas a-nochd d' fheòil-sa
fo thalamh reòthte Sròn Dhiùirinis
nuair ghlasas na coilltean sa Chèitean
èiridh do shunnd san t-sùghmhorachd.

The Burial of Sorley MacLean

27.11.1996

Your island under snow without you alive
was still as you had hewn it,
as people came to you in the church,
and the leave-taking was not unfitting,
for though you adhered to another order
the anguish was not dissimilar
of Christ in solitude in the Garden
and yourself on the height of the Cuillin.

Though I do not belong to your tribe
I give thanks to your mother,
to the Election that did not take you
one autumn day in the desert,
for the beauty of a face and an island,
for the music of the pipes and the language
in which you found a sense of heroism
and soothing for your people's pain.

Though you are locked below,
Sgùrr Alasdair is your headstone,
and far from the bounds of your country
your fists are raised against oppression;
though your flesh tonight will freeze
under the numb soil of Stron Durinish,
when the woods flush green in May
your mirth will rise in the sappiness.

MARK O. GOODWIN

Skye

Skye: I'm back again;
couldn't resist your wide horizon smiles
and the jewellery of your whitewashed houses
gummed to the summer-green glens and your sensuous
     coastal fringes.
Skye, I'm talking to you, can you hear me?
Only, you seem to be turning your back on me.
Sometimes you stare at me with your compound thistle eyes,
like some deadly insect, which scares me silly like leaning
     over a cliff edge.

Skye, are we falling out, or is it that we are spending
too long in each other's company . . .
Tha thu gam chur às mo chiall. You're driving me nuts.
Skye, are you clouding over again?
It cost me £14.70 to get here
and I seem to have had this conversation some place else before.
Will it rain again? Will it keep on raining? Will it ever stop?
Are the midges coming?
Will we ever get home together again?

Skye, I feel you have a single-track mind with no place to reverse:
we're a battleground of passing places.
You see, I try and make sense of you, understand your
     cultural sensitivities,
but forgive me, I'm a slow learner.
Eh! I was brought up in England,
fed on greed and nostalgic spoonfuls of Empire,
and now my feet keep sinking into your bogs.

MARK O. GOODWIN

An t-Eilean Sgitheanach

An t-Eilean Sgitheanach: tha mi air ais a-rithist;
cha b' urrainn dhomh do chraos-ghàire àicheadh
agus do thaighean geala mar sheudan
air an glaodhadh ri glinn uaine an t-samhraidh 's ri oirean
                              brìoghmhor a' chladaich.
Eilein, tha mi a' bruidhinn riut, a bheil thu gam chluinntinn?
Ach, tha thu mar gum biodh tu a' cur cùl rium.
Uaireannan spleuchdaidh tu orm led shùilean ioma-chluaranach,
mar bhiastaig mharbhtaich, a tha gam chur à cochall mo chridhe
mar gum bithinn a' lùbadh thairis air oir na creige seo.

Eilein, a bheil sinn a' dol a-mach air a chèile, no an e gu
                              bheil sinn ro fhada an cuideachd a chèile . . .
Tha thu gam chur às mo chiall. You're driving me nuts.
Eilein, a bheil thu a' fàs gruamach a-rithist?
Chosg e £14.70 faighinn an seo
agus tha e mar gum biodh an còmhradh seo air a bhith againn
                              am badeigin roimhe.
Am bi an t-uisge ann a-rithist? An cùm e air a' sileadh? An
                              dèan e turadh idir?
A bheil a' mheanbh-chuileag a' tighinn?
Am faigh sinn dhachaigh còmhla gu bràth a-rithist?

Eilein, tha mi faireachdainn gu bheil d' inntinn aon-shligheach 's
                              gun àite ann dhut dol air ais:
's e th' annainn blàr de dh'àiteachan-seachnaidh.
Bheil thu faicinn, tha mi feuchainn ri do thuigsinn, cùram do
                              dhualchais a thoirt fa-near:
ach thoir dhomh mathanas, tha mi mall gu ionnsachadh:
Eh! Chaidh mo thogail ann an Sasainn,
air mo bhiathadh air sannt agus spàintean cianalais na h-ìmpireachd,
's a-nis tha mo chasan a' dol fodha nad bhoglaichean.

God, you have so many bogs. All that water stored up there
for years, lacking minerals, and then what do you do?
Release the lot in a gush and guilt of waterfalls . . .
Skye – you obliterate me with your long nights
you turn my head with your sunsets
you make me dizzy with your giddy winds;
you know, sometimes they go on and on and on:
it's the only conversation we have for days,
and it drives me crazy.
And your bog myrtle perfume is making me ill.
I need a drink. More whisky. I haven't drunk enough of you yet.

Skye, let's put our relationship in some sort of order.
I know about the clan warfare, the Clearances,
the painful baggage of a previous marriage;
but can't we now tie our own individual Celtic knot with
      a little more hope?
Skye, you are not East Timor; Portree is not Dili.
I know, I know, it's not going to be easy:
crofting daughter is in trouble again;
she's being flattered with riches.
You've come over all postmodernist in Portree,
and Urban Nightmare, he stalks the shadows in the square
with the latest in mobile phone technology.

Locals are being barred from hotels in case we embarrass
      the guests.
Hey, where can I get a clootie dumpling this time of night?
Huh! Kilt Rock tilts, it's laughing at me. You bastard!
      You looking at me?
Ha, aye: I know what you're up to, standing there, pissing
      in the wind;

A Dhia, 's ann agaibh a tha na boglaichean. A h-uile boinne
                    uisge a tha sin air a stòradh,
airson bliadhnaichean, a dhìth mhèinnearan, 's an uair sin
                    dè a nì thu?
Leigidh tu às e ann an spùt is ciont de dh'easan . . .
Eilein – tha thu gam sgùradh às led oidhcheannan fada
ga mo chur tuathal led iomadh dol fodha grèine
gam fhàgail luaireanach le tuainealaich do ghaothan;
a bheil fhios agad, uaireannan leanaidh tu ort is ort is ort:
's e an aon chòmhradh a th' againn fad làithean,
's tha e gam chur às mo chiall.
'S tha cùbhrachd do roid gam dhèanamh tinn.
Feumaidh mi deoch. Tuilleadh uisge-beatha. Cha do dh'òl mi
                    mo leòr dhìot fhathast.

Eilein Sgitheanaich: dèanamaid seòrsa de dhealbh shlàn de ar
        càirdeas:
tha fios a'm mu chogaidhean cinnidh, na Fuadaichean,
an trom-uallach a ghiùlain thu bho phòsadh eile;
ach mach urrainn dhuinn a-nis ar snaidhm Ceilteach fhìn a
                    cheangal le beagan a bharrachd dòchais?
Eilein Sgitheanaich: cha tusa Timor an Ear; chan e Port Rìgh
                    Dili.
Tha fhios a'm, tha fhios a'm, cha bhi e furasta:
tha nighean na craite ann an càs a-rithist
ri linn brosgal a' bheairteis.
Tha Port Rìgh air fàs cho thar-ùr-nodha
agus Trom-laighe a' Bhaile-mhòir, e ag èaladh ann am
faileasan na ceàrnaig leis an teicneòlas fòn-làimhe as ùire.

Muinntir an àite toirmisgte bho thaighean-òsta air eagal nàire a
                    chur air na h-aoighean.
Haoi, càit am faigh mi clootie dumpling aig an àm seo a dh'oidhche?
Huh! Creag an Fhèlidh a' dol cam, a' magadh orm. A dhonais!
                    Bheil thu coimhead ormsa?
Ha, aidh: tha fhios a'm dè tha thu ris, nad sheasamh an sin, a'
                    mùn an aghaidh na gaoithe;

agus na lochain cho làn de dh'uisge, sùilean glainne stàrr-shùileach
   ris an oidhche.
Tha na fosailean air ghluasad a-rithist, cluinnidh mi na dìneasairean
   ag ionaltradh,
cluinnidh mi an ulfhart àrsaidh. Tha an làbha a' sruthadh.
Tha mi faireachdainn tinn. Uabhasach tinn. Duilich.
Tha mi duilich, tha mi air chall. I am lost.

Eilein, chan eil dragh gu bhith orm tuilleadh mu ar deidhinn.
                     Tha gaol agam ort. Bithidh gu bràth.
Tha fhios agad gu bheil mi ga chiallachadh, nach eil?
             Siuthad, can rium gun toir thu mathanas dhomh.
Tha an oidhche air a bhith fada. Tha an dithis againn sgìth. Tha
   mi a' tuigsinn.

Tha do nigheanan 's do mhic a' toirt dùbhlan dhut fhathast,
feuchainn ris an rud as fheàrr a dhèanamh dhaibh;
a' Ghàidhlig a chumail a' dol. A' chuid as fheàrr dhìot.
I'm sorry. Am faod sinn dìreach laighe sìos an seo
   le chèile, gu socair?
Cumaidh mi orm gad luaidh, tha mi 'gealltainn.
Èist ris na sailm a tha nan dust anns a' ghaoith.
   Dè nì mi? Dè nì mi?
Dè a nì mi mus sguab an ath chogadh sinn
dhan dorchadas, a' fàgail dìreach soillse reul os cionn
   Rubha Hùnais?
Sluigidh mi mo dheòir 's traoghaidh mi a' ghlainne 's
   ruigidh mi airson do thaobh caoin
's cuiridh mi bròg coiseachd air beulaibh na tèile –
tapadh leat, tapadh leat, tapadh leat.

. . . and those lochans so full of water, glassy eyes staring into
     the night.
The fossils are moving again, I can hear dinosaurs grazing,
I can hear the primordial howl. The lava's flowing.
I'm feeling sick. I am feeling very sick. Sorry.
Tha mi duilich, tha mi air chall. I am lost.

Skye, I am not going to worry about us any more. I love you.
     Will always.
You know I really mean it, don't you? Please say you'll
     forgive me.
It's been a long night. We are both tired. I understand.

You're still having a rough time with your sons and daughters,
trying to sort out what's best for them;
keeping the Gaelic going. The best part of you.

Tha mi duilich. Can we just lie down here together, quietly?
I'm going to keep on singing your praises, I promise.
Listen to the psalms that silt the wind. Dè nì mi? Dè nì mi?
What will I do before the next war plunges us
into darkness, leaving only the starlight to hover over
     Rubha Hunish?
I will swallow my tears and drain my glass and reach for
     your softness
and put one hiking boot in front of another –
tapadh leat, tapadh leat, tapadh leat.

iconic, that single mast, with the broad sail
and the high prow, and the oars dipping
in a rippling of sea and swash
a chronology of time and passage,
let us fathom the lesson of history.

there is the big
'if'
but we mustn't lose focus
we must be wary of the shoals that surround us
those rocks and sandbanks that trick us

the sail is hard to hoist in a heavy swell
so let's be clear about this
the government's level of financing has dropped
leverage is not easy to maintain

it is now or never
but to return to the relevant aspect of the situation
potentially it is big, very big
as wide as the horizon

the problem is trying to determine the outcomes
those blank sheets of possibility –
it is an unknown land
and the clouds are rolling in

but let us be clear about our vision
the mission that must be followed
it must be a good clean game
these things must be tested
with probity and prudence
so that everything is fit for purpose
for experience tells us, when it comes down to it,

that everything has its place, a bottom line,
the hard tacks of the task lie ahead –

let us learn the lesson of history
the way the Gael sailed in the swift birlinn
to the islands, to his port of call,
sea and bays charting the journey
until keels grooved the shore
and the land that was in him
was the land that he named

let us grasp the lesson of history
haul on the halyard

the landscape became the poem, the prayer,
humanity and its suffering etched
like a ridge across the brow of a headland,
the wind scoured for stories of lives
as it rushed over the water, over the machair,
over moorland of soft rush and sedge and cottongrass,
rattling the walls, rattling the doors, piercing the thatch,
howling to everyone to see for themselves
how dawn candled and cast its shadows.

RODY GORMAN

Ri Taobh Linne Shlèite

Choisich mi san uisge
Ri taobh Linne Shlèite
Nuair a dh'fhalbh thu san oidhche

'S dh'fhidir mi uisge-stiùireach
Is gun lorg idir air an t-soitheach
A dh'fhàg thall an sin e,

Sin agus a' ghealach
A' tuiteam an cridhe na beinne,
Fad' às, fann, sgàinte.

Air Bàs Charles Bukowski

'S e na dh' fhairich mi
Gun do chaochail Charles Bukowski

'S mi a' bruidhinn ris a' phost
Air a chuairt mar a b' àbhaist

A sgaoileadh nan litrichean 's nam pasgan
'S nam brathan-fios an-diugh sa mhadainn.

'S thàinig e dham ionnsaigh gun robh e fhèin
Ris a' phostaireachd uair a bh' ann

'S gum b' e fhèin a bha freagarrach
Seach am post air a bheil mi cho eòlach

A bhith romham an-diugh sa mhadainn
A' cur cuairt leis na litrichean

'S ag radh: *Madainn mhath — 's mi flìn am post ùr*
Agus chaochail mi 'n-dè

Ach mairidh mo chliù na mhìr
Bheag naidheachd mun chruinne-chè.

RODY GORMAN

Beside the Sound of Sleat

I walked in the rain
Beside the Sound of Sleat
After you legged it that night

And I noticed a wake
But not a trace
Of the vessel that left it there,

That and the moon
Falling in the heart of the mountain,
Faint, faraway, rent.

on the death of charles bukowski

i smellfeltheard that charles bukowski had changeoppositedied

*as i quarrelspoke to the pillarpostofficetrampman on his ceilidhpilgrimageround
comme l'habitude*

*scatterdelivering letters and littleflockbookpackages and
wordvisioninformationtreasonmessages this morning.*

*and it attackoccurcame to me that he himself was a lettercarryingtramp at one
hourtime*

*and would have been more accurateanswersuitable pastinstead of the
pillarpostofficetrampman i expertacquaintanceknow*

before me this morning on his letter ceilidhpilgrimageround

saying: morning – i'm thefairyoungfreshnewpillarpostofficetrampman
and i changeoppositedied yesterday

but my praisefamereputation will lastlive as a lightyounglittle lunchbit of
storynews aroundabout the creamspousenightworld

Ìomhaighean

'S e 'n t-saothair a chuir mi romham an-dràsta
Ìomhaighean a thoirt còmhla

De shaoghal an latha 'n–diugh
'S den àm a dh'fhalbh

Mar ìomhaigh
De Elle MacPheson, abair,

Is i mar Shìle nan Cìoch
Am meadhan *Mayfair*.

ghostcountenanceimagestatues

the diseasedmanpunishertidalislandbirthpainsouvre i've set myself just
now is to valuetastegivebring horndoortogether ghostcountenanceimagestatues

of today's livingageuniverseworld and of the seasontime that's gone

as a ghostcountenanceimagestatue of elle macpherson, talksay,

as sheila-na-gig-nave-tits in the waistcentre of mayfair

JAMES ANDREW SINCLAIR

Immigrant

Fill my pockets with lochs
the wind will fit snug in my wallet.
I will weave a scarf of mackerel, haddock and trout
the good fit of sheep on my feet.
My jacket, knitted peat and heather
with a bottle of good humour for the journey.
Planks of fishing boat bound tight as a belt
the sails making dandy trousers.
My back-pack holds the entire ocean
and last but certainly not least
i will wear the sky beneath my hat.

Makkin Hame

Charlotte Anne took da rodd her ancestors drave
strampin ower da hiecht o white-cappit waves
laek a flat stane skitterin ower da ream-calm.
Her sail filt tae da brim wi a nor-wasterd.
Fish room filt tae lipperin wi muckle codlin.

Bridders Jamsie; skipper an Willie wirkin da sail.
Jamsie's boys Geordie, an Mansie wha wis
named eftir his grand fedder. Da idder crew
Johnnie brucker, Sammy o Nort-Hoose an da
sheep tief's youngest boy; Daniel.

Willie wis watchin wadder, winderin earts
an takin meids as da mirkenin fell aa aroond. Jamsie
wis aa fur turning her heid in da wind, waitin morning licht.
Willie said naa, da wind wid turn southerly
an dey wid miss dir chance wi da tide.

Darkenin cam, an wi nae mön ta licht dir wey
dey reefed in da sail, doon-haulin wi wan easy pull
reducing canvas an haevin up da rackie on da tows.
Da speed fell aff Charlotte Anne as shu cam ta heel.
Willie ahint da stong, laid his haand on da halyard cleat.

Slippin aff his sea-buts an his ooie-socks
he set his twa cowld feet, een on da first swill
an wan on da second harsing.
Feelin da sea coorse trowe him, lik da blöd
in his veins, his hert pumpin fae da rush o da waves.

His lang taes, wirkin dir wey back and fore, ower
da splintery boards, laek fingers saftly wirkin
dir wey up da warm riggy-bane o a lass in a box bed.
Charlotte Anne plooed on, da mirr o da wind i da Stroods.
Aathing tick, slokkit in pitch an treacle.

Willie's een glinderin ta pick oot da moder-dye
taes feelin fur da heartbeat o a wirkin sixern.
Her thin skein streeched ower eddy an undertow.
A voice in his heid, da voice o his bridder
a lang lost ghost o eichty wan.

Caallin fae da deep. 'Nae guid'll come o dis, mak fur da nordert.'
An as dey med nort, he listened as Charlie's wirds faded awey.
Wi da dark cam da cowld, aabody happit up in whit claes dey hed.
Tinkin lang fur da chair afore da stove an warm bannocks.
Tryin herd no ta tink o da crabs gettin dir eyes.

Wi dat sam, Willie lookit ower an saw
a smudge o licht ta port, da Wasting
an ta starboard da sam, da hooses o Broch.
Listenin careful, fur da baa brak at da point
Willie yelled, 'Mak full helm ta port.'

As shu swang roond, he felt trowe his feet
da tide grippin da keel draggin her, racin
intae da soond. Willie pulled aff a lump o twist

pokkit hit in his pipe an strak a match.
'Nearly dere boys, drap da sail an grip da oars –

we'll be aroond da ness in a minute ur twa.'
An wi dat sam dey rowed, pullin her oot o da tide.
Dey saw lichts ashore, smelt paet reek
an dey aa let oot a a lang breath o relief, whin
da fore fit scraepit up da shingly beach.

PAMELA BEASANT

Visitors . . .
(for David Malouf, who dislikes the word 'vibrant')

. . . move through Stromness
unaware they are patching holes,
bumping ghosts; they touch
stone, thinking it's clean.

They find vegetables, good
coffee; they keep alive

take away atoms of sky
traces of accent, salt.

Sometimes one comes
with more absorbent
mind and eye.

For you, David,
I hope standing stones
brood by Aussie lagoons;
St Magnus's fat red pillars
prop the memory
of dappled tombs.

The autumn light (which is
not vibrant – never that)
was a little richer with you here;
is more various for you having
taken it home.

St Magnus Day
(for George Mackay Brown)

Shadow on the stone
echoes the angular jut of your chin;
fleetingly, you are everywhere,
except in the box being lowered down

and it's hard to leave you there,
to not look after you, bring blankets
for the cold, and soup to nourish, to show
that you had made it to another spring.

Old men weave a spell of death,
tangle in it willingly,
drop from the end of a history
that tries to breathe, and can't.

This will be the day we start to repeat
by heart the litany of a book slammed shut.

God and Magnus, Island, Hamnavoe,
squandered a feast of images through
one life; took you, feather-light,
left us circling the gap.

Exposed on ancient contours,
pinioned by an inexorable sky,
on this St Magnus day, we stand
at Warbeth, silent, where you lie.

Finding you in Rackwick

In Rackwick bay, stones are pink
with the effort of smoothing so much time
into perfectly flawed roundness.

They lie in a colony,
a petrified spawn of dinosaurs' eggs.
And from this distance the cliffs are tame,

postcard pretty. A fulmar
wheels from its nest,
tilts the world away from the sun.

A distant speck
jumps through the binoculars,
detaches from the steep and slatted rock,

becomes a little figure, running;
a tiny chaos making for an open shore.

JAMES KNOX WHITTET

Circles of Fire

They cannot conceive how it is possible for any
mortal to express the conceptions of his mind in
such black characters upon white paper: Martin
Martin, *A Late Voyage To St Kilda* (1698).

You brought the written word
to those islands where voices,
song and memory reigned to keep
the terrors of the dark at bay.

On luminous afternoons, the sundial
of rocks was caressed by time's restless
shadow; gannets exploded into mirrored
surfaces of bays beneath blizzards of cliffs.

On cupped evenings of summer
when Atlantic winds contained their
breath, fulmars floated above themselves
in shards of sunlight on suspended

wings, and the angular green fields
of corn were flecked with gold
between crossed stone walls, veined
with the orange dyes of lichens,

while, on the hill, the forefathers slept
beneath their coarse quilts of heather.
How could all of this be reduced
to scrawled lines on scraps of paper?

In Hirta's parliament where the
measured council of the elders' voices
rose above the Babel of the gulls,
there was no need for Hansard,

and in the Gaelic ballads, crooned
around the centered circles of fire
each night, the spoken word travelled
through mysteries of smoke to echo

beyond where ink could reach.

The Last Man on Jura

On those lucid Hebridean evenings
of summer when the branched antlers of stags
are mirrored on shifting lochans, weaving
reflections like drowning fingers; greylags
shadowing the sea's light, you gather driftwood
left stranded by tides, your arms raised,
annihilating those thoughts that gnaw your mind
down the long, stone corridors written with blood
to that numbered room where fear lurks to erase
undesirable meanings of the last man.

The Paps of Jura follow your every move
as peewits empty their bowls of liquid music
to fill the silence that stalks from the moor.
You return to Barnhill where the wick
of the single candle moves in its lighted dance
of the *ancient time* reviving ghosts
of the abolished past scented with fallen
bluebells before the mind's disciplined trance
by priests of fact who dam history's flow
until all that is real is a shared dream.

Afternoons, you lift brown trout from chocolate lochs,
whitened by anchored lilies; in the bay,
ringed with sounding whins, you lie back,
resting on nothingness, facing the sky
to count the constant number of held clouds
beyond the penal colonies of fiction

where words are trapped like ravenous rats in cages
and life laid flat in shelved, dusted records:
you drift on the slow waves' deviations
to some still untouched place where darkness is.

George Orwell wrote most of *Nineteen Eighty-Four*, originally entitled
'The Last Man In Europe', on the Hebridean island of Jura.

Words in italics taken from *Nineteen Eighty-Four*.

Moving with the Times

He sat in the back row of the classroom
drawing the faces of clocks, his blunted
pencil rounding a smudged penny, the drum
of rain sounding on the corrugated
roof, dates eroding at his fingertips.
In each separate circle, both short hands
would reach unsteadily to numbers scrawled
around the frayed circumference, his lips
pursed; engrossed in motions of time while strands
of weak sunlight, when the rain had ceased, sprawled

across distempered walls where maps, stained pink,
were stretched out between two pins. He was born
with a fault, his brain unable to link
his thoughts: a jigsaw with the pieces too worn
to fit. He worked on the croft, his mother,
widowed, took in men to stretch her income.
When moving woodwormed floorboards had settled
down for the night and the moon formed rivers
of light across faded linoleum
flowers, he'd listen as trapped sheep wrestled

with fences making tightened, barbed wires strum.
Mornings, in his black wellies, overturned

and greying, he'd shove barrowloads of dung
beneath wet, arched trees; on the loch, swans preened
their dark brood; above his bent head, white-fronted
geese arrowed for the ocean and left pale
reflections of themselves on stilled water.
A tractor brought mounds of clay into bleached
lines in fields where worms were upturned to veils
of gulls. In misted light, buzzards loitered

in moist gulfs of air. He died an old man
of twenty-seven, leaving behind heaps
of nameless jotters, their pages of worn
circles moving with the times. Those keepsakes
his mother burnt in a tidying fit
with ripped empty, yellow bags of hen feed:
dog-eared pages curled in flames extended
by stray breezes making flecks of ash flit
and rise and drawn, unsteady hands recede
as singed circumferences contracted.

Carousel of Silences

A pair of worn hands at rest on a black tweed
skirt: that is all there is to see. Yet those deep
veined hands with their broken fingernails
reveal not only a life but a way of being.

Those hands that have spun and woven and dyed
the clothes you, your husband, your children
and grandchildren wore are now fixed forever
in a held moment of stillness. You have woven

yourself and your loved ones out of time. In the
unseen cottage, hewn out of rock and weighed down
with boulders in defiance of storms, I imagine
a dark, walled clock with its spindly arms

folded as one onto the soft lap of noon.
Beneath echoes of time, on the beeswaxed dresser,
that carousel of silences: a china dog guarding each corner;
blue patterned plates and bowls; green whisky bottles;

the framed icons of the Virgin: her face, moulded
into serenity, glazed by veils of sunlight stealing
through hair-fringed window eyes. Outside, those uneven
pyramids of peat still glistening wet from deep layers

of moor where I see your bowed, shawled head shrouded
by midges. I catch that burnt honey scent of gorse
and picture black cattle daydreaming in mauves
of heather, ghosted by moist breaths of sea winds.

I see you also, bent double beneath a wicker
creel of seaweed, salt water streaming down your
back like smelting silver in afternoons of spring
with peewits preening and strutting between lazybeds.

A lifetime of joy and suffering scoured on hands
which you display with deep acceptance and pride as
if you sensed that you and your kind were the last
of a royal line with that crown of scythed, gold-flecked

oats in encircled stooks, angling across stoned fields in the
taken breath of a September evening, waulked by fingers of
moonlight, with green and silver bands of mackerel winding
beneath the translucent surface of the gouged eye of bay.

Those photographed hands live on like lived poems
while you, forever faceless, lie in the island's sparse soil.
The life of you and your kind like stories knitted
around a stubborn fire to keep the warmth within.

In 1954 the great American photographer Paul Strand spent three
months in South Uist and recorded a traditional way of life that was
soon to change. One of Strand's most haunting images consists simply
of a pair of aged hands resting on a faceless woman's knees.

IAIN S. MAC A' PHEARSAIN

na h-eilthirich is am BBC

shiud i
a' chailleach
àiteigin air a' Chladach a Tuath
air a glacadh mar ghiomach
anns an uisge
le muinntir a' BhBC

'dh'fhalbh iad,' ars ise,
'an fheadhainn òga;
's cha tig duine a chèilidh oirnn
tuilleadh.'

dualchas siùbhlach
cràdh an dealachaidh
am fianais sholas
is *mics*
is luchd-amhairc
ri dìdearachd thar a' chuain
a' cur sgleò nan linn
air aithris sliochd nan eilthireach

a' filmeadh sa bhaile iasgaich
far nach fhaigh thu tuilleadh iasg
ach bùth bheag
a reiceas rudeigin car coltach ris
clèibh ghiomach bheaga
mar chuimhneachan air an sgrìob

's an t-seann tè fhathast
an deas-meadhan na sràide
crogain *coke* ma cois
ann an tobar na cuimhne
a' caoineadh an t-sìl
a dh'fhalbh leis an uisge

'cut' 'nì sin an gnothach'

IAIN S. MACPHERSON

the emigrants and the BBC

there she is
the old lady
someplace on the North Shore
caught like a lobster
in the rain
by the folk from the BBC

'they've gone,' she says,
'the young ones;
and no one comes to visit us
anymore.'

a migrating heritage
the pain of separation
in view of lights
and mics
and spectators
peeping over seas
lowering the veil of ages
on the recitation of emigrant stock

filming in the fishing village
devoid of any fish
but a small shop
selling something like it
tiny lobster pots
souvenirs of the trip

and the old one still
in the middle of the street
coke cans at her feet
in memory's well
mourning the seed
that left with the rain

'cut' 'that'll do'

balbh an latha

mar chuimhneachan air Gilleasbaig Dòmhnallach, Tarsgabhaig

air latha do thiodhlacaidh
dh'èirich a' ghrian,
os cionn na bruthaich ud:
slàn, aghaidheach

is sheas Rùm is Canaigh
air beulaibh a' bhàigh,
mu choinneimh do thaigh':
coitheanal ann an eaglais bhàn

is seachad air a sin
an Cuilitheann air fad,
ceann-rùisgte:
mar dealbh calandair, buileach ùr

is nas fhaid' a-mach fhathast
na h-Eileanan Siar,
a thàinig am bàrr a dh'aona-ghnothach, cha mhòr:
air fàire, do-chreidsinneach clìor

agus air an rathad chuagach, lom
a-staigh dha do sheirbheis,
bha beanntan tìr-mòr nan seasamh mar chàch:
adan ceò orra sin, urram coimheach nad chòir

's dh'fhalbh na mionaidean oirnn,
mus deach do chur fon ùir
reòidhte, cho socair, cinnteach asta fhèin:
mar samhla ort, mar fhreagairt air balbhachd nan speur

still, silent day

in memory of Archie MacDonald, Tarskavaig

on the day of your funeral
the sun rose,
above that hill:
full, brazen

and Rum and Canna stood up
in front of the bay,
before your house:
a congregation in a vacant church

and beyond that,
the whole Cuillin ridge,
bareheaded:
like a calendar photo, brand-new

and out further still,
the Western Isles,
appearing almost on purpose:
on the horizon, unbelievably clear

and on the bare, bent road
in to your service,
the mainland mountains were upstanding like the rest:
wearing hats of mist, foreign honour in your midst

and the minutes stole away on us,
before you were set under the frozen
earth, so steady, sure of themselves:
like a symbol of you, like an answer to the still
                                        silence of space

Island Song

this island
with its membrane skies
    its skeins of light
    its skin-tight wind
    its strips of stretch-mark clouds

this island
with its pinprick larks
    its lapwing flap
    its swallow sweep
    its torn-out gull-shaped gaps

this island
with its salt-spray kiss
    its puckered waves
    its hungry shores
    its harkening and calling

this island
with its small dark holes
    its close-held cairns
    its ancient angst
    its blackness honed to silence

this island
with its whispered roads
    its singing hills
    its harboured howls
    its fanfare and its dirge

this island
with its bludgeoned sun
      its unkempt moon
      its scraps of stars
      its speckled universe

this island
breathing
in and out
in and out
like this

ANNA FRATER

Dà Rathad

Carson a bu chòir dhomh gabhail
na slighe ceart, lorn, fada?
Ged a tha an rathad air a bheil mi cam
agus tha na clachan a' gearradh mo chasan
agus tha dìreadh an leothaid
gam fhàgail gun anail,
chan e aon aon rud
a tha mise coimhead romham
latha an dèidh latha.
Agus shuas air an leathad
chi mi timcheall orm,
chi mi gu bheil barrachd ami dhòmhs'
na slighe cheart, fhada lom.

Tha thusa a' cumail do shùilean aor an' aon rud
ceart, dìreach air do bheulaibh
agus chan fhaic thu gu bheil an saoghal
ag atharrachadh timcheall ort.

Lit' Gun Shalainn

Sgian dubh 'na stocainn
agus Beurla na bheul;
moladh lit' sa mhadainn
's e cur muesli na bhòbhl;
'Chan fhaighear nas fheàrr na 'n t‑uisge‑beatha.'
Ach 's e Martini bhios e 'g òl . . .
nach ann truagh a tha'n cluaran
le boladh an ròis!

ANNE FRATER

Two Roads

Why should I follow
the long, smooth, straight road?
Although the road I take is crooked
and the stones cut my feet
and climbing the hill
leaves me breathless
I am not confronted
by the same prospect
day after day.
And up on the hill
I can see around me,
I can see that there is more in store for me
than a straight, long, smooth road.

You keep your eyes fixed on one point
right in front of you
and you cannot see that the world
is changing around you.

Unsalted Porridge

A sgian dubh in his stocking
and English on his tongue;
praising porridge in the morning
as he puts muesli in his bowl;
'You can't get better than whisky.'
But it's martini that he drinks . . .
isn't the thistle pitiful
when it smells of the rose!

Eilean Phabail

Mar thusa, tha mise
nam dhà leth;
a' seòladh air cuan
ach ceangailte ri creagan m' àraich;
uaine agus flùran;
a' sreap gu grian
agus nèamh;
creagan donn a' bàthadh
fo mhuir agus feamainn
agus dorchadas.

Faisg air daoine
gan coimhead,
gan cluinntinn,
ach cha ruig iad orm –
tha mi ro fhad' air falbh.
Chan urrainn dhomh fàgail,
chan urrainn dhomh tilleadh,
's cha tig an dà leth ri chèile.

Bayble Island

Like you, I am
divided,
floating on sea
but made fast
to my ground rock;
green and flowers
climbing to the sun and heaven;
brown rocks drowning under
brine and tangle
and darkness.

Near people,
watching them,
hearing them,
but they cannot reach me –
distance is maintained.

I can't leave.
There's no way back.
Halves remain separate.

BABS NICGRIOGAIR

An Gàidheal

'underneath the pavement there is the beach' — *may 68*

1

anns gach baile brònach
fon phavement fhiadhaich
tha tràigh gad ionndrain
bata na do làmh
bàta na do shùilean

2

neapaicin geal
mar isean air an iteig
an-dè aig a' phort-adhair
an-diugh na do phòcaid
tha an saoghal a' fàs nas lugha
's an taigh nas motha
tha a' chlann a' fàs mòr
gad fhàgail le fotos is telebhisean

ceann air balla neo air bocsa
ann an leabhar neo ann an sgàthan

cumaidh tu ort, le na soithichean 's le na sgòthan
an sian nad chùlaibh
seòladair nan speuran

3

eadar breith is bàs tha B&B ann an Glaschu
eadar prìs chaorach is prìs cruidh tha caitheamh-beatha
eadar clach is cladh tha cuimhne

BARBARA MACGREGOR

The Pakistani

'underneath the pavement there is the beach' — *may 68*

I

in every mournful city
underneath pavements growing wild
there is a beach that longs for you
a walking stick in your hand
a boat in your eyes

2

a white handkerchief
like a bird on the wing
yesterday at the airport
today in your pocket
the world is growing smaller
and the house bigger
the children are growing up
leaving you with photographs and television

a head on a wall or on a box
in a book or in a mirror

you will keep on with the dishes and the clouds
the rain at your back
sailor of the skies

3

between the births and deaths there is a B&B in Glasgow
between the price of sheep and that of cattle there is a livelihood
between a stone and a grave there is a memory

4

tha goirt san tìr
is pian nad amhaich
tha blas cànain
fhathast air do theanga
's an t-acras ort

5

le leac-uaghach an àite cluasaig
chan fhaigh thu mòran cadail

6

air do ghlùinean ann an cidsin
neo ann an achadh
ach seasaidh do chreideamh

4

famine is in the land
and a pain is in your throat
the taste of a language
lingers on the tongue
and you are hungry

5

with a tombstone for a pillow
you won't get much sleep

6

on your knees in a kitchen
or in a field
with your faith still standing.

An Duine Dubh

dachaigh air do dhruim
bùth air do bhaidhsagail
dh'fhosgladh tu do mhàileid
gàire làn grèine. 'Seall seo!'

lingerie an lingerbay
sìoda ann an làmhan cruaidh a' chroiteir
sìol ùr bho fad' às
cho aotrom, cho àlainn

a' siubhal am measg shrainnsearan
cothromaichte le feansaichean is cinn-theagaisg
cha robh nad cheum
ach cuimhne is cianalas
a' bàsachadh leis an fhuachd
reic thu d' aodach
's thog thu teine, taigh is teaghlach
an-diugh tha do bhùithtean làn dhaoine
's do mhàileid a' feitheamh
tha na làithean-saora a' fàs nas daoire
a-nis nach eil ach deilbh rin togail

The Highlander

a home on your back
a shop on your bicycle
you would open your suitcase
with a smile as wide as sunshine. 'Look at this!'

lingerie in lingerbay
silk in the rough hands of a crofter
new seed from far away
so light, so beautiful

travelling among strangers
weighted down by fenceposts and texts
only memory and homesickness
to dog your step
catching your death of cold
you sold your clothes
and you built a fire, a house and raised a family
today your shops are full of people
and your suitcase is waiting
the holidays are getting dearer
now there are only photographs to take

ALEX CLUNESS

Boat Song

This, I think, is like watching the disappearance and drowning return
Of a lamb rib, cracked and stirred and swirling to the surface
Then pitched down into barley broth and invisible in salt and scum.
And it may very well be that this boat, off to fish or to cages of fish,
Will be perfectly safe. But from where I stand it seems a hellish sea.
And rain really does roll down black island windows like tears.
For days like these are daguerreotypes of your whole life departed;
Silver halide bits and pieces and ghosts and spirits and the intermittent lights
Of that boat, or any boat, while all your waves and horses and boiling tides run
Vengeful and precarious for the rocks. Is it this price that makes you so bereft?
In the dark of the gowling glass, with the boat out of sight and the iodine breath,
There is no negative, no love, no history, and no destination southward left.

Moon

The blue moon swings by our side like a lantern, and has a shepherd's crook towards us;
The light from it is like the sun seen from swimming or when drowning underwater and
It belongs to another declaration different to this one, one earlier and before itself and new.
It belongs you know in a castle, broken apart with all its single-minded flags hauled down
High up in the mountains and the skies and snug up close to the sun where at noon dainty
Heralds will shout out the truth about life, and no one in the valley will want to listen.

Doppelgänger

I think you resemble someone gone forever. And it is like the sea we hear, falling down the sky.
You say it is an upside down sea this island. It is an endless horizon aching with blue and sun.
It is a twist somehow in the perception. Rather like being seated with you at this table now and
Knowing that these are not the words you are saying. I am at the edge of a different sea again.
You are no longer before me, but you are before me now. Writing, you are writing with a pen.

Lighthouse

There is a lighthouse orange and it signals the time when this is this and that is that.
The western sun will die graceful above her blue Calvary. It is destiny and we applaud.
It's just not good to pretend beyond what's real; there is no ladder to the end of this.

There is a lighthouse orange and it signals from the black and blue face of the sea.
Laughter is contorted in the dark, but we know it is still you outside, mad living.
The moon has a fullness never seen; there is no ladder to the end of this.

The Fisherman

The fisherman
Given over to love
Began a carving
When the days rolled less:

To bless this Madonna
And baby saviour
He kissed the finished piece
As the North Sea
Squeezed the concertina
Of their fragile red boat

My girl
He said to himself
Is more important to me
Than I can ever know
I must just trust to God
That she is safe

The ocean formed a landslide
And at a wild angle
The call came to haul the nets

LISE SINCLAIR

Kuna

Dunna speak my neem ower da haaf
Traet me aes da fraemd, lat nuy
Shadow-toitht o me cut dee boo

Even spaekin peerie-wyes hit mitht caa
Coors wadder abut dee heid, mitht pit
Swell apo tide, an flaow dy gunnel ower

Aes da lines I baited airlier d'duy
Drap doon glintin an sharp wi hoop
Dy haunds'll fill wi fysh

An du makks on at dat sem haunds
Dunna keen da hedd o me aes du hauls
Me fae sleep, weel

A'll preeve nuy sic unkenness wi dee
Here be da banx, da rigg, da brigg-steen
Ur beyd, I tak dee be nuy idder neem

Du is ut deyr, cauld
Markin meaðs on dat shiftin world

Yit draan braeth
Fae da sem staur-turnin nitht

KUNA da fyshermans' sea neem/taboo neem fur wife/woman
KONA (Icelandic)
KUNA (Jacobsen)

LISE SINCLAIR

Kuna

Don't mention my name on the sea
Show no recognition, let no
Shadow-thought of me cross your bow

Even a whisper might bring the storm
Around your head, might add
Swell to tide, and flow your gunnel over

As the lines I baited earlier today
Drop down glinting and sharp with hope
Your hands will fill with fish

And you pretend that these same hands
Do not know the hold of me, as you pull
Me from sleep, well

I suffer no such denial of you
Here at the cliff, the rigg, the door-stone
Or bed, I accept you by no other name

You are out there, cold
Placing absolutes on that shifting world

Yet drawing breath
From the same star-turning night

KUNA is the Fair Isle fisherman's sea name/taboo name for woman.
KONA (Icelandic)
KUNA (Jacobsen)

Harmonium/Granny

Hamnavoe, circa 1974

The harmonium has no out-breath but a song
Bellows yawn and roll I remember as your feet
Pedal that steady music-less beat
And you breathe air
Into the harmonium lungs

Meanwhile the hymn
Swells and soars over my head
And you're singing
      'Will your anchor hold
        in the storms of life?'
As if God was asking you himself

I didn't know then but do now
That yours had held, somehow
Steadfast and sure while
Outside the window the seasons shifted
Again and again the strong tides lifted
The pier thronged and fell quiet
Boats left and came home prayed for
Foula, sons and brothers disappeared
And appeared from under blue squalls

And you, bustling round your harmonium
Eyes fixed on that other bright horizon
Flour dusted from your bannock-baking hands
Floating chords on the ivory air

Suddenly at the door, stark with constellations
Of fisherman's-gensey-stars
Fish-boxes and old haddock-ends
Grandad comes in with the bass:
      'Grounded firm and deep . . . '

The storm of life is every day
Angry waves threaten and breakers roar
Surges rave and wild winds blow
But this music is yours
You will not drown

Only lately, long after
You'd passed it on to me, this
Harmonium-shaped love
When memory became your home
And the present a complete stranger
You told me how
Your first year at the gutting in Lerwick
Your knife flashing red through herring
Was preserved and stowed
Surer than the fish – a transformation
Cold-salt wages into this
Same, longed-for harmonium
Bought second-hand from a place
– now the Marlix – sixty years on

MARK RYAN SMITH

Unsindered

(D Sailor's Haumcumin)

Man an wife,
lang held sindree –
d rowl an d rise an d ebb o
thoosands apu thoosands o
waves lyin atween.

Sho maaks apo hir sock,
watchin hit grow;
d sam as Penelope tinkin lang
aboot hir man scuddin an rumblin
awaa aboot d wide oot-yunder.

Rowlin oot doa fir banniks.
Maakin eenyauch fir dm baith.
A herd habeet t brak.
Sho slides d banniks ida oavin an,
untinkin, trivvils d herd lent u d
owld rowlin preen.

A stoor o baaky ida keetchin,
ungkin an ert kent baith tgidder,
pooz hir itae d present tense.
An a voys – coorsind we saat an rum an d
cumpinee o iddir meyn –
spaeks hir name, clear eenyauch.

Shu aupins d oavin doar
an smiles as sho sees d
banniks rizn up boanie.
He draaz fae his pipe,
spaeks naun but staands we a blyde look
whin he seez d haet banniks staandin
prood, foo an tiftin.

Rejoined

(*The Sailor's Homecoming*)

Man and wife,
long held apart –
the roll and the rise and the fall of
thousands upon thousands of
waves lying between them.

She knits,
watching the garment grow;
the same as Penelope thinking yearningly
about her man crashing
around in the wide ocean.

Rolling out dough for scones.
Making enough for them both.
A hard habit to break.
She slides the scones in the oven and,
absent mindedly, fingers the hard length of the
old rolling pin.

A smell of tobacco in the kitchen,
both strange and well known at the same time,
pulls her into the present tense.
And a voice – made coarse with salt and rum and the
company of other men –
speaks her name, clear enough.

She opens the oven door
and smiles as she sees the
scones have risen pleasingly.
He draws on his pipe,
doesn't speak any more but stands looking happy
when he sees the hot scones standing
proud, full and swelling.

Mark Ryan Smith   229

Emigration

Scotland,
folded like a paper cone,
funnelled its folk to this place.
Glasgow became the hinge;
on either side lives swung.
The gangway lay waiting
to lift feet from native land;
arms, like the last strands of root
at hairst, held to those left wondering
if they had been right not to go.
Letters would come,
with words moving east, to home,
and west, to hope.
America:
can you ever box the compass?
can you ever make the broken parts whole?

CHRISTIE WILLIAMSON

Burns

Da sun shone trow
da skylicht
an da lang caald
haet sten
bruised me taes
wi firgottin dreams.

Oo an feddirs
an boady haet
kept dat coarnir
o hoose at my hert
fae bein is caald
is da air.

A haund, a pyjamaed airm
oge itae da moarneen
pu socks onta itchy feet.
Tay sarks an jumpers
ir shocked on in wan, leegs
shiver inta breeks.

I pick up da dry
chamber pot, creak
my wye oot da door
an lat me smucks
grip ivvery step
ta brakkfist.

Da röf I slept aneath is gien,
da lumb'll nivver reek;
bit whaarivvir I wakk
da fire my graundfeddir set fir me
it da boddom o da stair
'll low athin me banes.

Haundline

Dippin aneath da rip
o a new mön tide
phosphor sings
wi da driftin kyiss
o a staurlit waltze.
Da grund opens,
waves whisper
sweet sometheens

tae smooth necks,
ticklin da bellies
o selkies wi fingirs
dancin cheek ta cheek,
da sang giein leegs
ta waek heids
nibblin aa nicht
on da huik at glistens
aneath da boo.

JEN HADFIELD

Simmerdim

The sun shows where it intends to rise.
This is the state of the light:
the low hill has plumped up like a loaf,
the road to North Roe sunk dough-deep.

I wish I were the one whose cuticles
are simmerdim, his light smudged lead,
whose promises are full of false summits.

My light is trapped by cattle-grids
and the road's white stitches.
Headlamps waken cats' eyes.
Then the moor falls blind again.
I bend to touch the closed lids.

Simmerdim. Pushes downy heat
into crowns of Collafirth and Ronas,
is ticks and whiskers
and tail-barbs vibrating for a mate.
Its tallow is a curlew's cry –
no call as brash as my torch in this sky –
it has a thousand bubbly pulses
gurgling
            go-go-go-to-bed.

Where I walk a hedgehog freezes,
every grey snaps shut,
each pale withdraws.

Crying Taing

The peat is cherried with thick water.
I lever out bones like almonds.
From the grass I pick bones like butterflies
with moor-coloured bone-circled eyes.

From bones like orchids, pan-pipes, fans,
I build the ewe kicking out last night at cars
and the small leap of Ronas Voe;
today blood-muzzled, blind.

I pick up a fragment
for every bone in my body.
My fingers as cold as the bones in the grass.
I wind them round a panhandle, a pen.

Blashey-wadder

At dusk I walked to the postbox,
and the storm that must've passed you earlier today
skirled long, luminous ropes of hail between my feet
and I crackled in my waterproof
like a roasting rack of lamb.

And across the loch,
the waterfalls blew right up off the cliff
in grand plumes like smoking chimneys.

And on the road,
even the puddles ran uphill.

And across Bracadale,
a gritter, as far as I could tell,
rolled a blinking ball of orange light
ahead of it, like a dungbeetle
that had stolen the sun.

And a circlet of iron was torn from a byre
and bowled across the thrift.

And seven wind-whipped cows
clustered under a bluff.

And in a rockpool,
a punctured football reeled around and around.

And even the dog won't heel since yesterday
when – sniffing North addictedly –
he saw we had it coming –

and I mean more'n wet weak hail
on a bastard wind.

Snuskit

The shore is just not nice. Good. The hashed basalt is black and all the rubberduckery of the Atlantic is blown up here – a bloated seal and sometimes skull, fishboxes and buoys, a cummerbund of rotting kelp. The wind topples me, punches me gently into a pool. Beyond, strafed with hail, the sea teems like TV, with frayed aerial. I step back onto my tuffet, boots pooled in buttery light. The wind punches me gently into a pool. I'm doing my best impression of a gull – pesky, pitied, lonely, greedy, hopping up and down on my tuffet. The wind punches me gently into a pool.

Hedgehog, Hamnavoe

Flinching in my hands
this soiled and studded but *good* heart,
which stippling my cupped palms, breathes –

a kidney flinching on a hot griddle,
or very small Hell's Angel, peeled from the verge
of a sweet, slurred morning.

Drunk, I coddle it like a crystal ball,
hellbent the realistic mysteries
should amount to more than guesswork

       and fleas.

PÀDRAIG MACAOIDH

Làmhan Rùisgte

Tha Dòmhnall air ais à Iorag le làmhan rùisgte
gun sgeul air fhàinne-phòsaidh, gun ghuth
air na thachair a-bhos.
    Tha am feise bàn
ach chan eil Ceit a' gearan, le sùil fear nam pìoban
ga bioradh fhathast na bruadar. Na
throm-laighe bidh Dòmhnall a' luasgadh
agus ag èigheach mu dheidhinn salchar
agus fuil; na dhùisg cha bhi e ag ràdh
smid.
    Tha an fhàinne chùldaich mar tost
eatarra; nuair a thig a chàirdean chan eil bòst
no dibhearsain na bhreugan. Chan eil ach fàsach
na shùilean.
    Tha Ceit a' cur seachad
lathaichean san leabharlann, a' sgrùdadh naidheachdan
aosta à Iorag. Chan eil ach dìochuimhne sna pàipearan
agus seachnadh, chan eil ach àireamhan
neo-ionnan agus sanasan-reic.
    'Haditha',
sin uile na thubhairt e an oidhche ud, mus deach e a-mach
ri uthachd, no ri smuain agus ath-smuain
a' ghnìomh, ri taobh na mara làin,
a làmhan dearg san fhuachd. Ach
tha làn-fhios aig an dithis aca
nach robh e riamh faisg air an àite.

PETER MACKAY

Naked Hands

Donald is back from Iraq with naked hands,
no sign of his wedding ring, no word
of what happened over there.
    The sex is pale
but Kate doesn't complain, with the piper's eyes
still boring her in her sleep. In
his nightmares Donald turns
and shouts about dirt
and blood; awake he says
nothing.
    The lost ring is a silence
between them; when his friends come there is no boast
or fun in his lies. There is only desert
in his eyes.
    Kate spends
days in the library, scanning old news
from Iraq. There is only forgetting in the papers
and avoiding; statistics,
disagreement and adverts.
    'Haditha',
was all he said that night, when he went out
to suicide, or thought and the thought
of the act, beside the full sea,
his hands red in the cold. But
they are both fully aware
he was never near the place.

An Tiona

Nuair a bha mi sa bhunsgoil
fhuair mi tiona sleamhainn tana
far an cuirinn m' fhaclan
sgrìobhte air sgoltaidhean pàipeir.

Chan eil cuimhne agam air inneach
ach air cho doirbh 's a bha e fhosgladh
gun ainmearean 's gnìomhairean a' leum
a-mach às mar bhradain à lìon –

iorghail bhalbh mo chànain
a' snàmh gu sìorraidh gu dachaigh chaillte.
Nam cheann tha an tiona air meirgeadh,
's cha tèid fhosgladh gun bristeadh saillte.

Logorrhoea

Bu tu gaol òir m' òige
do ghàire ghaoil mar fhir-chlis
an geamhradh gorm Leòdhais
mo ghaol, mo rìbhinn òg.

Nan robh mi nam fhear-iomchair
's chan e fear-bholg, fear-cuideachd,
bhithinn air tairgsinn gaol maireannach
an àite logorrhoea

agus a-nis tha mo ghaol aig tèile
mar bu chòir 's mar bu dual,
ged a tha do sholais nam speuran
a' lainnireadh thar a' chaoil.

The Tin

When I was in primary school
I got this thin-walled tin
where I'd stash my words
writ on splinters of paper

I can't remember the design
but how difficult it was to open
without names and deeds leaping out
like salmon from a net

the dumb babble of my languages
swimming forever towards their lost ground
the tin in my head rusted not to be opened
without breaking its crust of salt.

Translated by Ciaran Carson

Logorrhoea

You were the gold love of my youth
your laugh love like the northern lights
in the blue Lewis winter
my love, my young love.

If I was a bearer,
not a waster and follower,
I'd have given you lasting love
in place of logorrhoea.

Now my love's another's
as is right, as should be
though your lights are in my skies
glittering across the kyle.

RAMAN MUNDAIR

Stories fae da Shoormal *

I

Here. Hear da ice craack.
Be still. Wir forever
on da move. Dis rodd
gengs naewye, dis rodd
gengs aawye. Da onnly
thing daat truly flaows is da sea.

Da sea lonnlie, da sea,
da sea seduces, da sea,
da sea screms, da sea,
da sea senses, da sea,
da sea, da sea. In me drems

der a rodd it gengs on
laang, laang – forever. Unlichted,
un-shadowed, I canna see
mysel bit I kyen, Ah'm dere. Un-alon,
awaash o me, awaash o midnicht
blue. Da skies waash ower me.

Da ice craacks, da Arctic tundra
shivers, readjusts hits spines,
sends secret messages idda dialect
tae hits nerve-endins in Shetlan.
Dir ley lines here
vibratin, crackin – electric.

* *Shoormal* (Shetland dialect) – the place where the sea meets the shore

RAMAN MUNDAIR

Stories fae da Shoormal

I

Here. Hear the ice crack.
Be still. We are constantly
on the move. This road
goes nowhere, this road
goes everywhere. The only
thing that truly flows is the sea.

The sea lonely, the sea,
the sea seduces, the sea,
the sea screams, the sea,
the sea senses, the sea,
the sea, the sea. In my dreams

there is a road that continues on
long, long – forever. Unlit,
un-shadowed, I cannot see
myself but I am there. Un-alone,
awash of me, awash of midnight
blue. The skies wash over me.

The ice cracks, the Artic tundra
shivers, readjusts its spines,
sends secret messages in dialect
to its nerve-endings in Shetland.
There are ley lines here
vibrating, cracking – electric.

Strange hoo far awa
memories come tae be – laek waves
laevin da shore
Wha wis da wumman?
Wha wis da man?
We met idda da shoormal
Dee. Dee. Dee.
Du wis my fire
wance – My man
o' da waves. Du cam,
rested upo my shore.
I wis dy first
I wis dy harbour.
Bit my love, my selkie
Man, du wis
        run agrund. Ach,
siccan a sad thing for a sailor.
An noo my love da sea
is my rodd, da rodd my sea.
I traivel on for my love
wisna meant tae be.
        Da ocean,
    da waves,
da shoormal –
    dis is noo my place,
my warmin space, my
    restin, my faimily.

2

Strange how far away
memories become – like waves
leaving the shore
Who was that woman?
Who was that man?
We met at the shoormal
You. You. You.
You were my fire
once. My man
of the waves. You came,
rested upon my shores.
I was your first
I was your harbour.
But my love, my selkie
Man, you were
        run aground. Ach,
such a sad thing for a sailor.
And now my love the sea
is my road, the road my sea.
I travel on for my love
was not meant to be.
    The ocean,
    the waves,
the shoormal –
    this is now my place,
my warming space, my
    resting, my family.

ROSEANNE WATT

Haiku

The scarecrow's pumpkin face
smiled at me last summer
now he is sneering.

CONTRIBUTORS

JOHN ABERDEIN was born and brought up in Aberdeen, and his award-winning novels *Amande's Bed* and *Strip the Willow* centre on that city. His stories were edited by Duncan McLean in *Ahead of Its Time*. He lives and writes in Hoy.

MEG BATEMAN, born in Edinburgh, teaches at Sabhal Mòr Ostaig in Skye. She has co-edited and translated three anthologies of Gaelic medieval, seventeenth-century and religious verse. Her own poetry collections, *Aotromachd/ Lightness* and *Soirbheas/ Fair Wind,* were shortlisted for the Scottish Book of the Year in 1997 and 2007.

PAMELA BEASANT was born and brought up in Glasgow. She moved to Orkney in 1986, where she has been working as a freelance writer and editor. She has been widely published as a poet and non-fiction writer, and was the first George Mackay Brown fellow in 2007. Publications and commissions include *Running with a Snow Leopard* (Two Ravens Press), *Orkney: A Celebration of Light and Landscape* (with photographer Iain Sarjeant), *Stanley Cursiter: A Life of the Artist,* and three scripts performed at the St Magnus Festival, for whom she is director of the Orkney Writers' Course.

NORMAN BISSELL lives on the Isle of Luing in Argyll and writes poetry and non-fiction. He graduated in philosophy and history from the University of Glasgow, was a principal teacher of history and then an Area Officer of the Educational Institute of Scotland. He collaborates with musicians and visual artists and his poetry collection *Slate, Sea and Sky: A Journey from Glasgow to the Isle of Luing* (with photographs by Oscar Marzaroli) was published in 2008. He is director of the Scottish Centre for Geopoetics: www.geopoetics.org.uk.

GEORGE MACKAY BROWN (1921–1996) was born in Stromness, Orkney, which remained his lifelong inspiration. He studied in Edinburgh, where he met Edwin Muir. In 1941 he was diagnosed with tuberculosis and lived an increasingly reclusive life in Stromness. But in spite of his poor health he produced a stream of work from 1954 onwards, including the 1994 Booker Prize-shortlisted *Beside the Ocean of Time*.

RHODA BULTER (1929–1994) was born in Lerwick, Shetland. After her first poem was published in *The New Shetlander* in 1966, she grew to become one of the most prolific and popular of the Shetland poets. Her collections are *Shaela*, *A Nev Foo A Coarn*, *Link-stanes* and *Snyivveries*. She also recorded three collections of her poems, which are now available on CD. She was much loved for her sense of humour and vigour, and contributed regularly to Radio Shetland.

AONGHAS PÀDRAIG CAIMBEUL/ANGUS PETER CAMPBELL is from South Uist. He attended Garrynamonie Primary School, then Oban High School, where his English teacher was Iain Crichton Smith. He graduated in Politics and History from the University of Edinburgh, where he was taught by Sorley MacLean from Raasay and Professor Richard Ashcraft from California.

MAOILIOS M. CAIMBEUL/MYLES CAMPBELL comes from Staffin, Isle of Skye, where he now lives. He has published six collections, the first in 1980, plus a co-authored collection, and his work is widely anthologised with English translations. He is a part-time distance learning tutor with Sabhal Mòr Ostaig.

ALEX CLUNESS was born in Aberdeen. His poetry is collected most recently in *Mend* and *Disguise*. He edited *The New Shetlander* for a time.

EDWARD CUMMINS (1944–2005) was born in Sydney, Australia. He was an oral poet. During his lifetime very little of his poetry was published in the ordinary way. He lived in Orkney for a time. After his death friends collected his works and they have now been published under the title *I Flame at Words*.

GORDON DARGIE was brought up in Lanarkshire. He taught English, first in Lanarkshire and Argyll, and from 1980 in Shetland where he and his wife still live after his retirement as Principal of Shetland College. In 2009 Kettillonia published his first collection, *a tunnel of love*.

IAN HAMILTON FINLAY (1925-2006) was born in Nassau in the Bahamas. After his family returned to Scotland, he left school at 13 and attended Glasgow School of Art briefly before wartime service. His artistic life encompassed poetry, philosophy, history, gardening and landscape design – all fully realised in his famous garden, Little Sparta. After a lifetime of spats with authority (particularly the Scottish Arts Council), aged seventy-seven he accepted a CBE.

ALISON FLETT was born and bred in Edinburgh but lived in Orkney for eleven years before moving to Australia. Her collection of poetry, *Whit Lassyz Ur Inty*, was shortlisted for the Saltire First Book of the Year Award. She is currently working on her second novel.

ANNA FRATER/ANNE FRATER was born on the Isle of Lewis. Her first language is Gaelic and her poetry has been published in *Fo'n t-Slige* and various anthologies and magazines. Married with two children, Anne lives in her native village of Pabail Uarach and is a lecturer on the UHI Gaelic degree courses at Lewis Castle College.

MARK O. GOODWIN was born in Devon and moved to Skye in 1994. He is co-author of the collection *Dà Thaobh a' Bhealaich/ The Two Sides of the Pass*. His poem 'Skye' was selected for the Scottish Poetry Library's Best Scottish Poems in 2009.

RODY GORMAN À Èirinn. Am measg nan cruinneachaidhean leis tha *Zonda? Khamsin? Sharaav? Camanchaca?*; *Chernilo*; *Eadar Fiaradh is Balbh na h-Oidhche* agus *Beartan Briste*. Air a bhith na sgrìobhadair còmhnaidheach aig Sabhal Mòr Ostaig, Oilthigh Chorcaigh, Oithigh Mhanitoba agus PROGR (Bern). Na fhear-deasachaidh air an iris bhàrdachd *An Guth*.

LAURENCE GRAHAM (1924–2008) was born in Stromfirth, Shetland, in 1924. A part-time crofter for most of his life, he was also active in local politics. After WWII he studied in Edinburgh and then took up several teaching posts in Shetland, which he combined with joint editorship (with his brother) of *The New Shetlander* from 1956 to 1988. In 2000 Shetland Library published a volume of his selected poems.

YVONNE GRAY was born in Ayrshire and moved to Orkney in 1990. She lives near Stromness. She enjoys collaborations with other writers, musicians and visual artists. Her poems have been published regularly in magazines and anthologies and her first full collection, *In the Hanging Valley*, was published in 2008.

ANDREW GREIG was born in Bannockburn. He is a full-time writer of novels, 'life writing' and poetry collections. His latest works are *At the Loch of the Green Corrie* and *Getting Higher: The Complete Mountain Poems*. He lives in Edinburgh and Orkney, which for many years has been a significant part of his life.

MAVIS GULLIVER spent many holidays in the Hebrides before being appointed to the headship of the primary school on Colonsay in 1991. Since retiring she has lived on Islay, where she writes in a log cabin on the shore of her garden.

JEN HADFIELD lives in Shetland. Her first collection *Almanacs* was written in Shetland and the Western Isles in 2002, and it won an Eric Gregory Award in 2003, which enabled her to work on her second collection, *Nigh-No-Place*, in Canada and Shetland. She went on to win the T. S. Eliot Prize for *Nigh-No-Place*, which was also a Poetry Book Society Recommendation as well as being shortlisted for the Forward Prize for Best Collection.

ROBERT ALAN JAMIESON was born in Shetland, where he grew up, and is the author of a number of books of poetry and fiction, most recently *Nort Atlantik Drift* (2007) and *Da Happie Laand* (2010). He is currently a tutor of Creative Writing at the University of Edinburgh.

LAUREEN JOHNSON belongs to Voe, Shetland, and co-edits *The New Shetlander* magazine. She has written poems, stories, plays, non-fiction and a short novel. Her poetry pamphlet *Treeds* was published in 2007 and reprinted in 2010.

CHRISTINE DE LUCA was born and brought up in Shetland. She is a prize-winning poet, with five collections written in both English and Shetlandic. Her most recent is *North End of Eden*. She has had poetry published in many languages and won the poetry Prix du Livre Insulaire 2007.

DÒMHNALL MACAMHLAIGH/DONALD MACAULAY was raised on the island of Great Bernera, Lewis. He published his first volume of Gaelic poetry *Seòbhrach ás a' Chlaich* in 1967. He has held a number of senior academic posts, including a professorship in the Celtic Department at the University of Glasgow. He edited the influential *Nua-Bhàrdachd Ghàidhlig/ Modern Scottish Gaelic Poems*.

PÀDRAIG MACAOIDH/PETER MACKAY is a writer, academic and broadcaster. He has published a pamphlet of poems, 'From Another Island', with Clutag Press, and a critical study of Sorley MacLean. He is originally from the Isle of Lewis, and has lived in Glasgow, Barcelona, Dublin and Belfast.

HUGH MACDIARMID (1892–1978) was born in Langholm. He trained to be a teacher, spent many years off and on as a journalist, served in the medical corps during WWI, and founded the National Party of Scotland. A champion of the Scottish language for linguistic and political reasons, he spearheaded the Scottish Renaissance of the twentieth century and was, interestingly, a modernist and a communist. His book-length poem, *A Drunk Man Looks at the Thistle*, is considered to be one of the most important in twentieth-century literature.

SOMHAIRLE MACGILL-EAIN/SORLEY MACLEAN (1911–1996) was born on the island of Raasay. He studied in Edinburgh, fought in North Africa during WWII and taught in several schools, with a long spell as rector at Plockton High School. He was a highly influential figure at the heart of the Gaelic renaissance in Scotland and his work addressed great injustices, from the Highland Clearances to Rwanda, as well as love.

MORAG MACINNES is Orcadian, but has also lived in Shetland, Germany and Lincolnshire, where she worked as a community artist and lecturer. Her poems and short stories have been published in various places over the years. Most recently Hansel Cooperative Press published *Alias Isobel*, a verse narrative in dialect.

ALASTAIR MACKIE (1925–1995) was born in Aberdeen. Following active service in the Mediterranean during WWII he attended Robert Gordon's College and graduated from Aberdeen University with a First in English. He taught English at Stromness Academy, before settling in Anstruther until his retirement in 1984. After juvenilia he began writing in Scots (on which his reputation rests) in 1954 but continued from time to time to write in English. He was regarded, along with Robert Garioch, as the outstanding Doric poet of his time, with a tough-minded European aesthetic. His principal publications are: *Soundings* (1966); *Clytach* (1972); *Back-Green Odyssey* (1980); and *Ingaitherins*.

AN T-URR. IAIN MACLEÒID/REV. JOHN MACLEOD (1918–1995) was born in Arnol, Lewis. He served in the Royal Navy during WWII and, in 1948 in Canada, married Dolena MacKenzie from Stornoway. His poems and articles appeared regularly in *Gairm* and other publications, and for many years he was a Gaelic columnist for *The Oban Times*.

TORMOD MACLEÒID/NORMAN MACLEOD (1904–1968) was born in Portvoller, Point, Lewis. His mother was the seventh daughter of a seventh daughter. After his education he taught in a succession of Lewis schools and took particular interest in the language, folklore, literature and music of the Gael. He was an enthusiastic contributor to *Gairm*. His work ranges from delicate short lyrics to ferocious satire.

AONGHAS MACNEACAIL is an award-winning poet, journalist and broadcaster. Although writing mostly in English and Gaelic, he also shared the 2010 MacCash Prize for a poem in Scots. He writes song lyrics (for others to sing) and has read in the UN building, New York, Newfoundland, Seattle, Japan and on the Capitol in Rome, among other venues.

IAIN MAC A' GHOBHAINN/IAIN CRICHTON SMITH 1928–1998) was born in Glasgow to parents who had left Lewis to seek work. After the family returned to Upper Bayble, his widowed mother struggled in poverty and he never forgot this time. He went to university in Aberdeen and, following National Service, started teaching in Clydebank and then Oban. His first novel, *Consider the Lilies*, came out in 1968 and was preceded (and followed) by a stream of remarkable poetry, short stories, other novels and plays.

IAIN S. MAC A' PHEARSAIN/IAIN S. MACPHERSON was born in Alberta, Canada. Of Hebridean descent, he came to Skye in 1996 and lectured in Gaelic at Sabhal Mòr Ostaig until 2006 when he moved to the University of Ulster. Besides poetry he makes documentaries for BBC ALBA on subjects from the fur trade to emigration from the Western Isles.

RUARAIDH MACTHÒMAIS/DERICK THOMSON was born in Lewis. A renowned academic as well as a poet, he was Professor of Celtic at the University of Glasgow from 1963 to 1991. He was a founding editor of the Gaelic language periodical *Gairm* and he brought into being Comhairle nan Leabhraichean, the Gaelic Books Council, in 1968. He was elected a Fellow of the Royal Society of Edinburgh and of the British Academy.

JIM MAINLAND is from Shetland, where he teaches English at Brae High School. His collection *A Package of Measures* was published in 2002 and his poetry and prose can be found in various anthologies, magazines and online.

JIM MONCRIEFF was born in Lerwick. A regular contributor to *The New Shetlander*, his poems feature in several Shetland publications including two collections of his own, *Seasonsong* and *Beaten Gold*. Jim died in 2010. A new selection of his work is planned.

EDWIN MUIR (1887–1959) was born on the Orkney island of Wyre. His family relocated to Glasgow in 1901, a traumatic move for Muir. Within a few years both his parents and two of his brothers died, and Muir found himself alone in the city. After working in a number of menial jobs and becoming involved in left-wing politics he began contributing poetry to magazines. He met his future wife, Willa, in 1918; she would later become a well-known novelist. They travelled extensively through Europe in the 1920s and 1930s; symptomatic of a rootlessness that would never leave Muir. His first collection of poetry was published in

1925 and he became a central figure in the modern Scottish literary renaissance. In 1950, now Warden of Newbattle Abbey College, he encouraged the early writing of George Mackay Brown. He died in Cambridge in 1955 and is buried nearby.

RAMAN MUNDAIR is an artist and the author of *A Choreographer's Cartography, Lovers, Liars, Conjurers and Thieves* and *The Algebra of Freedom*. She is a Rolex Mentor and Protégé Award nominee, a Robert Louis Stevenson Award winner and was identified recently by the BBC/Royal Court Theatre as one of the 'next generation of promising new writers in Britain'.

DONALD S. MURRAY comes from Lewis but works in Shetland. A full-time teacher who is also a poet, author and journalist, his books include *The Guga Hunters, Small Expectations* and *And On This Rock: The Italian Chapel, Orkney*. His latest book is *Weaving Songs* (Acair).

BABS NICGRIOGAIR/BARBARA MACGREGOR was born on the Isle of Lewis and is a native Gaelic speaker. She is a peace activist and has worked in writing, visual arts, broadcasting and theatre. Her work appears in *Wish I Was Here* (edited by Alec Finlay and Kevin MacNeil).

CATRÌONA NICGUMARAID/CATRIONA MONTGOMERY was born on the Isle of Skye and educated at Portree High School, the University of Glasgow and Jordanhill College of Education. She was the first writer in residence at Sabhal Mòr Ostaig, the Gaelic college on Skye. Her work is widely anthologised and her full-length collection is *Rè na h-Oidhche*.

MÀIRI NICGUMARAID/MARY MONTGOMERY was born in Arivruaich in the Isle of Lewis. She was educated at Balallan School, The Nicolson Institute in Stornoway, and the University of Aberdeen. Two of her books were published by Coiscéim in Ireland, and two by Acair in Stornoway. She lives in Balallan.

MÒRAG NICGUMARAID/MORAG MONTGOMERY was born and raised in Roag, Dunvegan, on the Isle of Skye. She has written for television as well as print media and her work features in *Gairm*, the anthology *Sruth na Maoile* and *A' Choille Chiar*, a joint collection by Morag and her sister Catriona.

SIÙSAIDH NICNÈILL lives on Skye and teaches Gaelic medium primary. Her work is included in a number of anthologies; her collection *All My Braided Colours* was published by Scottish Cultural Press. She is currently working on a series of paintings and poems with Scottish landscape artist Pam Carter.

ALISTAIR PEEBLES came to Orkney with his family from Edinburgh in 1985. Editor of *OAR* from 1989 to 2002, he founded Orkney Writing Fellowship in 1997 and the GMB Fellowship in 2006. He is a writer, photographer and publisher (of Brae Editions), currently researching the early career of Ian Hamilton Finlay.

ALISON PRINCE has written biographies of Kenneth Grahame and Hans Christian Andersen, and among other prizes won the Guardian Children's Fiction Award and the Literary Review Grand Poetry Prize twice. She holds an honorary Doctorate of Letters for services to children's literature and has published two poetry books.

SHEENAGH PUGH is originally Welsh. She visited Shetland for many years and now lives there. She is retired and formerly taught Creative Writing at the University of Glamorgan.

JACK RENWICK (1924–2010) was a poet and writer from Unst; a major contributor to *The New Shetlander* from its inception in 1947, he wrote traditional and satirical verse in English and Shetlandic.

T. A. ROBERTSON ('VAGALAND') (1909–1973) is widely regarded as one of the greatest Shetland poets of the twentieth century. Raised in Westerwick and Stove in Waas, he adopted the old Norse name for the area as his nom-de-plume. After studying at the University of Edinburgh he became a teacher in Lerwick. In 1945 he founded the Shetland Folk Society and was an office bearer until his death. He was also instrumental in establishing *The New Shetlander*.

JAMES ANDREW SINCLAIR began writing in his forties. He published a pamphlet of poems 'Gulf Stream Blues' through North Idea in 2007. James's poems have appeared in various magazines. He has read his work at Word–fringe and Wordplay book festivals. James is on the editorial committee of *The New Shetlander*.

LISE SINCLAIR is a poet/songster/crofter from Fair Isle and the music and language traditions of the Northern Isles. Lise also writes music, notably a suite of Shetland poetry settings: 'Ivver Entrancin Wis'. Other work includes: *Under the Evening Sky*; *White Below*; *Empty Ocean* and *here*.

MARK RYAN SMITH lives in Shetland with his wife and two daughters. His poetry, fiction and critical writing have appeared in *Gutter Magazine*, *Glasgow Herald*, *The New Shetlander* and *PN Review*. *Midnight and Tarantella*, a poetry pamphlet, was published in 2008. He is currently a part-time PhD student at Glasgow University.

IAN STEPHEN is a storyteller, poet and artist from the Isle of Lewis. In 1995, after fifteen years of service in the Coastguard, he became a full-time writer. Stephen was awarded writing bursaries from the Scottish Arts Council in 1981 and 1995. He was also the inaugural winner of the Christian Salvesen/Robert Louis Stevenson award.

STELLA SUTHERLAND was born in Bressay. She writes poetry in both English and Shetland dialect. Her collections are *Aa My Selves: Poems 1940–1980*, *A Celebration and Other Poems* and *Joy o Creation*. She has recorded some of her poems on the cassette tape *Driftwood Chair*.

WILLIAM J. TAIT (1918–1992) was born in Shetland. He studied English at the University of Edinburgh and became a teacher, working in England and later Dundee. While living in Edinburgh he was a member of the famous group of writers who gathered in Milne's Bar. After briefly joining the Communist Party he helped to revive the Shetland Labour Party and also founded the journal *The New Shetlander*.

ROSEANNE WATT has spent a good part of her two decades of life living in the village of Sandwick in Shetland. She is studying English Literature and Film and Media at the University of Stirling.

JAMES KNOX WHITTET was born and brought up in Islay. He edited the anthologies *100 Island Poems of Great Britain And Ireland* and *Writers on Islands*. His collections include *Poems from The Hebrides*. He won the Neil Gunn Award in 2009.

CHRISTIE WILLIAMSON was born in Lerwick, spending his first years in Westsandwick before moving to Mid Yell aged six. He writes poems in the language of Shetland and in English. *Arc o Möns* was published by Hansel in 2009. He lives in Glasgow.

ACKNOWLEDGEMENTS

We are grateful to the following for permission to reproduce copyright material.

Faber & Faber Ltd for the poems 'Childhood', 'Houses', 'The Northern Islands', 'An Island Tale' and 'The Swimmer's Death' by Edwin Muir from *The Complete Poems of Edwin Muir*; Carcanet Press Ltd for the poems 'Perfect' and 'Shetland Lyrics' from *Collected Poems* and 'In the Shetland Islands' from *The Islands of Scotland* (Batsford) by Hugh MacDiarmid; Mrs Dolina Gunn for the poems 'Raoir chunna mi'/'Last night I saw' and 'Bàgh Leumrabhaigh'/'Lemreway Bay' by Norman MacLeod; Shetland Museum & Archives for the poems 'Kwarna farna?'/'Where are you going?' and 'Water-lilies' by T. A. Robertson ('Vagaland') from *The Collected Poems of Vagaland* (The Shetland Times Ltd); Carcanet Press Ltd for the poems 'An Roghainn'/'The Choice', 'Ban-Ghàidheal'/'A Highland Woman', 'Am Bata Dubh'/'The Black Boat', 'An t-Eilean'/'The Island', 'Coin is Madaidhean-allaidh'/'Dogs and Wolves', 'Tràighean'/'Shores', 'Am Mùr Gorm'/'The Blue Rampart', 'Reothairt'/'Spring Tide' and 'Hallaig' by Sorley MacLean from *Collected Poems*; Brian Tait for the poems 'Fat Marget's Ballade' and 'The Gift (1949)' by William J. Tait from *A Day Between Weathers: Collected Poems 1938–1978* (Paul Harris Publishing); Hodder Ltd for the poems 'Hamnavoe', 'The Old Women', 'Hamnavoe Market', 'Old Fisherman with Guitar', 'Beachcomber', 'Winter: An Island Boy' and 'Peat Cutting' by George Mackay Brown from *Collected Poems* (John Murray); Derick Thomson for the poems 'An Loch a Tuath'/ 'The North Loch (Broad Bay)', 'Tha Mirean nan Rionnag 'nam Chuimhne'/'I Recall the Twinkling of the Stars', 'Fàgail Leòdhais, 1949'/'Leaving Lewis, 1949', 'Pabail'/'Bayble', 'Làraichean'/ 'Ruins', 'Clann-nighean an Sgadain'/'The Herring Girls', 'Aig

Tursachan Chalanais'/'At Callanish Stones', 'Am Bodach-Ròcais'/ 'The Scarecrow' and 'Leòdhas as t-Samhradh'/'Lewis in Summer' from *Creachadh na Clarsaich* (Macdonald); Mary Graham for the poem 'Flans Frae Da Haaf' by Laurence Graham from www.shetlanddialect.org.uk; Jim and Liz Sutherland for the poems 'High flyer' and 'Winter comes in' by Jack Renwick from *The Harp of Twilight* (Unst Writers' Group); Stella Sutherland for the poems 'Aesy for Some', 'At da Croft Museum' and 'Da Time and Da Tön' from www.shetlanddialect.org.uk; Frances Mackie and Kate Wood for the poem 'Three Tree Poems' by Alastair Mackie from *Ingaitherins: Selected Poems* (Mercat Press); Carcanet Press Ltd for the poems 'Tha thu air aigeann m' inntinn'/'You are at the bottom of my mind', 'Owl and Mouse', 'The Clearances', 'The White Air of March (1)', 'Poem of Lewis', 'Old Woman' and 'Nothing will Happen' by Iain Crichton Smith from *Collected Poems*; Pia Smig of Wild Hawthorn Press for the poem 'Orkney Interior' and extracts from 'Orkney Lyrics' from *The Dancers Inherit the Party and Other Poems* (Polygon), and 'Blossom Quarry, Rousay' and 'Voyage' from *Ian Hamilton Finlay: Selections* (University of California Press) ed. Alec Finlay; Dorothy Stove and John Bulter for the poems 'Shetlandic' from *Link-Stanes* (The Shetland Times Ltd) and 'Bül My Sheep' from *Shaela* (Thuleprint Ltd) by Rhoda Bulter; Donald MacAulay for the poems 'Fèin-Fhìreantachd'/ 'Self-righteousness', 'Soisgeul 1955'/'Gospel 1955' and 'A' Cheiste'/'The Question' from *Seòbhrach ás a' Chlaich* (Gairm); Alison Prince for the poems 'Rough Sea' from *Having Been in the City* (Taranis Books), 'Hens' and 'Having no Cattish'; Mavis Gulliver for the poem 'From one island to another' first published in *Envoi* 156, June 2010; Birlinn Ltd for the poems 'oideachadh ceart'/'a proper schooling' and 'gàidheal san eòrp'/'a gael in europe' from *A Proper Schooling and Other Poems* (Polygon), 'tiodhlac feirge'/'the gift of anger' and 'am fìor mhanaifeasto'/ 'the real manifesto' from *Hymn to a young demon* (Polygon) and 'home' from *Rock and Water* (Polygon) by Aonghas MacNeacail;

Jim Scott for the poem 'Buckie Man' by Edward Cummins; Myles Campbell for the poems 'Eileanan'/'Islands' from *Eileanan: Poems* (Department of Celtic, University of Glasgow), 'An t-Eilean na Bhaile'/'The Island a Town' from *Bailtean* (Gairm), 'Dà Ghuth'/ 'Twa Voices' from *A' Càradh an Rathaid* (Coiscéim) and 'Bàrd Baile?'/'Village Poet?' from *Saoghal Ùr* (diehard); John Aberdein for the poems 'Yesnaby' and 'Orkney Movement' first published in *OAR 5* (Orkney Arts Society); Luath Press Ltd for the poems 'Slate, Sea and Sky', 'Sounds' and 'To Take a Boat Out' by Norman Bissell from *Slate, Sea and Sky*; Christine De Luca for the poems 'St Ninian's Isle' from *Plain Sang* (Shetland Library) and 'Viking Landfall' and 'Paet Wark' from *Voes & Sounds* (Shetland Library); Amy Moncrieff and Alex Cluness for the poems 'Slow to Return' and 'Time to Dream' from *Beaten Gold* (New Dead Language) and 'Cutting Corn' from *Seasonsong* (Shetland Library) by Jim Moncrieff; Catriona Montgomery for the poem 'Sireadh'/ 'Seeking' from *A' Choille Chiar* (Clò-Beag); Laureen Johnson for the poems 'Staandin sten' from *Circles and Tides* (Skeklers Theatre Company) and 'Shore skippers' from *Mindin Rhoda* (Shetland Folk Society); Morag MacInnes for the poems 'A Masterpiece of Amazing Realism', 'Mrs Orkney interviewed' and 'The Superhero in Scotslit: a submission for my Masters' (a version of which appeared in *Navigating Home*, GMB Fellowship); Morag Montgomery for the poem 'Geamhradh'/'Winter'; Sheenagh Pugh for the poems 'Days of November 2009' first published in Poetry Scotland, 'Come and Go' first published in *PN Review* and 'Dresden Shepherdesses of 1908' first published in *The New Shetlander*; Gordon Dargie for the poems 'At Bannaminn: voar' and 'At Bannaminn: hairst' from *A Tunnel of Love* (Kettillonia Press); Bloodaxe Books Ltd for the poems 'Shetland', 'Orkney/ This Life', 'Stromness Evening' and 'Papay' by Andrew Greig from *This Life, This Life* (Bloodaxe); Jim Mainland for the poems 'Avoiding the Mitford Sisters', 'A Child Lifts the Shell of the World to her Ear' commissioned by the New Shetland Museum and Archives, 'Prestidigitator' from *Bards in the Bog* (Shetland Library), 'The Devil's Music' from *A Package of Measures* and 'The Gunnister Man' from http://sheenaghpugh.livejournal.com/; Alistair Peebles for the poem 'Burn' from *Turning Space: Five Versions of February* (Brae Editions); Angus Peter Campbell for the poems 'Geàrraidh na Mònadh à Smeircleit'/'Garrynamonie from Smerclate', 'Eòin', 'I Love You' and 'Ag Iasgach a' Mhic-Meanmna'/'Fishing the Imagination' from *One Road* (Cànan) and 'The Magic Clock' from *The Greatest Gift* (Fountain Publishing); Siùsaidh NicNèill for the poem 'Iona, West Beach on a Rainy Day' from *All My Braided Colours* (Scottish Cultural Press); Mary Montgomery for the poems 'Baile Ailein'/'Balallan' and 'An Taigh-Tasgaidh 's an Leabhar'/'The Museum and the Book' first published in *Gairm*, winter 1973; The Windfall Press for the poems 'I'll Boil the Kettle' and 'Bothy – Taransay Island' by Ian Stephen from *Providence II* (Windfall Press); Donald S. Murray for the poems 'The Girl Who Taught The Fisherman To Read' from *Between Minch and Muckle Flugga* (Kettillonia Press), 'Language' from *Small Expectations* (Two Ravens Press) and 'Ness Social Club, Fivepenny Machair' from *West-Coaster* (Cuan Ard Press); Yvonne Gray for the poems 'Cragsman' from *Mailboats: Playing with Wind and Tide* (Handsel Press) and 'Nousts' from *In the Hanging Valley* (Two Ravens Press); Luath Press Ltd for the poems 'Glunta (A fisherman's prayer)', 'Shore Poem' and 'T' Scallwa Castle' from *Shoormal* and 'Frisk Waatir Troot' from *North Atlantic Drift* by Robert Alan Jamieson; Meg Bateman for the poems 'Iomallachd'/'Remoteness' and 'Tiodhlacadh Shomhairle MhicGill-Eain'/'The Burial of Sorley MacLean' from *Lightness and Other Poems* (Polygon); Mark O. Goodwin for the poem 'An Tìr'/'The Land'; Two Ravens Press for the poem 'Skye'/'An t-Eilean Sgitheanach' by Mark O. Goodwin from *The Two Sides of the Pass*; Rody Gorman for the poems 'Ri Taobh Linne Shlèite'/'Beside the Sound of Sleat', 'Air Bàs Charles Bukowski'/'on the death of charles bukowski' and 'Ìomhaighean'/'ghostcountenanceimagestatues' from *Fax and Other Poems* (Polygon); James Andrew Sinclair for the poems 'Immigrant' from *Bards in the Bog* (Shetland Library) and 'Makkin Hame' first published in *The New Shetlander*; Pamela Beasant for the poems 'Visitors . . .' from *Navigating Home* (GMB Fellowship anthology), 'St Magnus Day' and 'Finding you in Rackwick' from *Running with a Snow Leopard* (Two Ravens Press); James Knox Whittet for the poems 'Circles of Fire', 'The Last Man on Jura' and 'Carousel of Silences' from *Poems from The Hebrides* (Island Press) and 'Moving with the Times' from *100 Island Poems* (Iron Press); Iain S. MacPherson for the poems 'na h-eilthirich is am BBC'/'the emigrants and the BBC' from *Wish I Was Here* (pocketbooks) and 'balbh an latha'/'still, silent day'; Alison Flett for the poem 'Island Song'; Anne Frater for the poems 'Dà Rathad'/'Two Roads', 'Lit' Gun Shalainn'/'Unsalted Porridge' and 'Eilean Phabail'/'Bayble Island' from *Fon t-Slige* (Gairm); Babs NicGriogair for the poems 'An Gàidheal'/ 'The Pakistani' and 'An Duine Dubh'/'The Highlander' first published in *Edinburgh Review*, spring 1998; Alex Cluness for the poems 'Boat Song', 'Moon', 'Doppelgänger' and 'Lighthouse' from *Mend* (New Dead Language) and 'The Fisherman' from *Disguise* (Kettillonia Press); Lise Sinclair for the poems 'Kuna' and 'Harmonium/Granny' from *White Below* (Hansel Press); Mark Ryan Smith for the poems 'Emigration' first published in *Gutter* magazine and 'Unsindered/Rejoined'; Christie Williamson for the poems 'Burns' (commissioned for Hidden Tramway event, 2008) and 'Haundline' first published in *The New Shetlander*; Bloodaxe Press Ltd for the poems 'Simmerdim' and 'Crying Taing' from *Almanacs* and 'Blashey-wadder', 'Snuskit' and 'Hedgehog, Hamnavoe' from *Nigh-No-Place* by Jen Hadfield; Peter Mackay for the poems 'Làmhan Rùisgte', 'Naked Hands', 'An Tiona'/'The Tin' and 'Logorrhoea' from *From Another Island* (Clutag Press); Raman Mundair for 'Stories fae da Shoormal (1) and (2)' from *A Choreographer's Cartographer* (Peepal Trees Press); Roseanne Watt for the poem 'Haiku'.

GRATITUDE

Wholehearted thanks to: Neville Moir, Judy Moir, Alison Rae, the Saison Poetry Library at the South Bank Centre, Edward Crossan, Sarah Morrison, Vikki Reilly, Alex Cluness, Donald Anderson, Peter Urpeth, the Scottish Poetry Library, Mark Smith, Alec Finlay, Alistair Peebles, Luke Allan, Robert Alan Jamieson, Donald S. Murray, Norman Bissell, Alex MacDonald, Seonaid MacDonald and all the writers whose poetry is included in this volume.

A NOTE ON THE EDITOR

Kevin MacNeil is a multi-award-winning writer originally from the Isle of Lewis. A widely acclaimed novelist, poet and play-wright, his books include *A Method Actor's Guide to Jekyll and Hyde, Love and Zen in the Outer Hebrides* and *The Stornoway Way*. He has held a number of prestigious writing residencies in Scotland and other countries and has lectured in Creative Writing at universities such as Edinburgh and Uppsala. MacNeil has collaborated with visual and musical artists, notably with singer-songwriter William Campbell. A keen bike-rider, he cycled along 1,300km of the River Danube on a fixed-gear bike through four countries in a dozen cycling days, raising money for two cancer charities. He is working on a new novel, a travelogue and a drama.

kevinmacneil.com